THE SMALLER HOME

D1210808

THE SMALLER HOME

CREATING THE PERFECT FIT

Dan F. Sater II, A.I.B.D

COLLINS|DESIGN

An Imprint of HarperCollins*Publishers*

Davie County Public Library
Mocksville, North Carolina

THE SMALLER HOME: CREATING THE PERFECT FIT

Copyright ©2006 by COLLINS DESIGN and DOLEZAL & ASSOCIATES

All rights reserved. No part of this book may be used or reproduced in any manner whatsoever without written permission except in the case of brief quotations embodied in critical articles and reviews.

For information, address Collins Design, 10 East 53rd Street, New York, NY 10022.

HarperCollins books may be purchased for educational, business, or sales promotion use.
For information, please write:
Special Markets Department, HarperCollins*Publishers*, 10 East 53rd Street, New York, NY 10022

First paperback edition published in 2008 by:

Collins Design
An Imprint of HarperCollins*Publishers*
10 East 53rd Street
New York, NY 10022
Tel: (212) 207-7000
Fax: (212) 207-7654
collinsdesign@harpercollins.com
www.harpercollins.com

Distributed throughout the world by:
HarperCollins*Publishers*
10 East 53rd Street
New York, NY 10022
Fax: (212) 207-7654

Conceived and produced by Dolezal & Associates, Livermore, California

Library of Congress Cataloging in Publication Data
Sater, Dan F.
    The smaller home: creating the perfect fit / by Dan F.
Sater II.--1st ed.
        p. cm.
    ISBN-13: 978-0-06-089189-3 (hardcover)
    ISBN-10: 0-06-089189-0 (hardcover)
1. Small houses--United States. 2. Architectural design. I. Title.
NA7205.S28 2006
728'.370973--dc22
                                    206004254

ISBN: 978-0-06-156532-8

Printed in China.

3 5 7 9 8 6 4 2 Printing, 2008

The contributors and credits on pages 170–173 are hereby incorporated in the content of this page.

Contents

Introduction

Designing a new custom home or remodeling a house to adapt it to changing needs can be a challenging project. At times, either process can even be overwhelming. However, if they are done properly and with careful thought, building or remodeling a house can be the most rewarding project of your lifetime.

In my nearly 30 years of residential home design experience, I have guided many clients on these wondrous journeys past many pitfalls as they planned and built their dream homes or adapted residences to better fit the way they lived. Along the way, I have seen both success and failure. In this book, I will share the fruits of my experience in these real-world situations and offer tools to ensure that you have a positive, pleasant experience, whether you build a new home or remodel one.

I will also provide you with numerous tips, examples, and evaluation worksheets designed to keep you from becoming your own worst enemy as you envision your dream home and all its features. In the past, some of my clients relied on comfortable but outdated conventions, such as following one-room/one-purpose thinking or dedicating space for once-a-year guest visits or parties. Others, enticed by magazines and home shows, confused desires with needs or suggested design options that would have led to needlessly oversized homes with the characters of an ill-fitting suit.

Opposite A home can be smaller than its counterparts even as it retains all their luxurious appeal and feel. The smaller home is endowed with great construction materials, craftsmanship, and detailing. An optimum balance of space and functionality is found when the smaller house is also *smarter*–when it establishes new levels of efficiency, reaps cost savings, provides optimum traffic flows, and maximizes its potential by using labor-saving and other beneficial technologies to make it the easiest and safest home in which you and your family can possibly live.

I'll also dispel the notion that building a smaller home means you have to give things up and settle for less. Nothing could be further from the truth. A house that closely fits your needs is smarter and better than its larger counterpart, even as you make decisions to reduce it in scale.

Looking at the physical processes and the psychological and emotional factors that influence our thoughts will help every home builder and remodeler avoid impulsive or obsessive behaviors that too easily take over and rule important decisions. It may seem strange to discuss psychology in a book like this, but a clear understanding of these fundamental factors is essential to the your understanding of the home design process.

What is it that makes other people insist on having more bedrooms than they really need or including spaces that will rarely be used? Such extras consume money and other resources, robbing them of comfort and enjoyment in your primary living needs. Instead, learn from their mistakes and bypass any tendency towards excess. You'll find help here to make healthy, beneficial planning choices.

When I think of my favorite smaller and smarter homes they bring to mind thoughts of classic beauty and timelessness. These homes share timeless design elements that create:

- relationships in harmony with both their owners and sites
- purposeful spaces that flow together yet interact to create a singular presence
- appearances that are at once soothing and exciting

This book will help you embark on your home-design journey while avoiding detours and keeping an eye on your ultimate destination: an ideal house and home.

Like many journeys, your trek to the perfect house is one of self-discovery, often filled with both frustration and exhilaration, but—in the end—well worth your trip.

I hope this book will also help you create a smaller home that embodies these values and more, reflecting your character, tastes, and—more importantly—how you truly live in your home. After all, it's not the size of your home that matters, but the quality of life it will provide you. May your journey bring you home!

Dan Sater

Opposite **A smaller and smarter home—such as the one seen here, featured on the cover, and profiled as the same plan at a different location in Chapter Three—is filled with purpose, promise, and its owners' needs. To the outside world, it portrays classic values and invites inspection of its details. It achieves its goals of minimizing size while remaining gracious in appearance and using space efficiently. Inside and out, such houses are not better simply because they are smaller and smarter, they are smaller and smarter because they are planned to fit their owner's needs.**

Necessity Meets Function

I once had clients who wanted an exercise room adjacent to their master bedroom and asked that I include it in their new home's plans. They were in love with fitness and expected to use the room every day.

The lot was tight. Balancing the client's wishes for convenient workouts with a desire to give each room a view meant the exercise room didn't rate a position by the master suite. I located it in a walk-out basement. It still had a view, but it remained quite far from the master.

When my clients saw it there, they said it just wouldn't do. "Why?" I asked. They replied, "It's too far away. We'd have to walk down the stairs and climb back up every time we used it."

Combining two rooms eventually gave my clients their exercise room, but the irony of the contradiction has stuck with me. Our wishes may not always be practical, but we'll find many more solutions if we understand our needs and consider how we live in our houses.

———

A challenge to anyone planning to build or remodel a smaller home is making the house fit their family's complex, often-changing needs. It's common to dream of a home with many specialized rooms, though they may be unrealistic and impractical.

Opposite The great room of this Rehoboth Beach, Delaware, home embodies many of the desirable features of a smaller and smarter home. A favorite location for many activities, it combines function with grace and charm. The window wall of slider doors gives full access to the covered porch from the room, leading to a grand entry stairway from the street.

Like the would-be fitness enthusiasts, everyone focuses on the features they want in their new house. You might imagine cooking in a professional kitchen, while another dreams of soaking placidly in a spacious, quiet tub. A few may want a master suite with a morning kitchen and sitting room, a retreat where they can withdraw from the world and all its responsibilities. Others are practical hobbyists who enjoy such activities as sports, sewing, or woodworking. Whatever the dreamers' desires, homes seem to pop into mind equipped with dedicated spaces to enjoy them.

At the same time, it's common to focus in on an existing house's shortcomings. You begin a chorus of disenchantment: "Our apartment's too small, too noisy, and the walls are too thin." … "You can't turn around in the kitchen." … "There's no place to fold the laundry when it comes out of the dryer." The list goes on and on.

Whether the problem is a crowded dining room at Thanksgiving or the sound of banging pipes from an overworked plumbing system, the remedy is often to move or renovate. A new home or remodel will fulfill every dream and eliminate all the defects…or so you hope and plan.

Your imagination fills with a mixture of wishes, recognized drawbacks, and possible solutions to each problem you perceive. Thoughts swirl as you attempt to set priorities and choose where to start. Your dreams would come true if only there were unlimited space and an infinite budget.

But common dreams and considerations of limitations are generalities. For success, it's important to think specifically. The key to planning a new, smaller home is balancing your hopes with complete knowledge about your current house.

Where to Start?

A good strategy is to pull back and really understand how it was once possible to live in your house with all its positive and negative features, how you live in it right now, and how your preferences would change for living in it or its replacement tomorrow. From this perspective, you will view your home, its rooms, and its amenities in a new light. You'll be able to add features and space for tasks and activities you like and reduce the amount of space taken by those you don't. This is a powerful new way to mentally stretch and squeeze your house's structure in ways that would be quite impossible to do for any real home's walls, floor plan, or features, so take full advantage of it while you are still in this hypothetical stage of planning. To help, use a worksheet to order your thoughts (see A Lifestyle Survey, page 16.)

Opposite **The front stairs and porch of the home first seen on page 10 is welcoming to guests and passersby. Its overhead sundeck and columned sitting areas are not just inviting but practical– they offer additional living space through three seasons.**

Above **An adjacent window suggests architectural boundaries for a casual dining area opposite the kitchen. Smaller homes require flexible space. The table, chairs, and area rug seen here give way to other furnishings and uses of the area.**

Above The V-shaped island with a double sink and opposite-side seating makes the 13-by-15-foot (4-by-4.6-meter) eat-in kitchen ideal for entertaining. The kitchen has ample space and multiple workstations suited to a pair of cooks preparing meals as they engage in conversation with friends and family. (See previous pages 10–13 for other views of the house).

Duvall Street

Rehoboth Beach, Delaware. Sater Design Group

A mixture of Key West conch and island influences gives this 2,123-square-foot (197-square-meter), two-story home a captivating curbside appearance. Just 26 feet (7.9 meters) wide, the house suits its long and very narrow lot. The home's exterior—reflected as well within its walls—features horizontal siding, fish-scale shingles, arches, and dormers. A functional upstairs sundeck and a lower deck expand the living space to outdoor areas.

A 10-foot (3-meter) ceiling downstairs allows for extra storage in cabinets, and use of practical elements and finishing details give the house a feeling of space while retaining full functionality.

Left The master bath features a his-and-hers vanity, whirlpool tub, stone facings, and column-and-arch trimwork frame windows that spill sunlight throughout the day.

Bottom left A pair of gables with arches below them and a recessed dormer behind repeat an architectural theme from the house's front on its rear face. The windows make full use of the nine-foot bedroom ceilings upstairs.

Below Recessing the back door on the side of the house beneath a covered porch makes the kitchen quickly accessible from the driveway. A covered deck, sheltered under an overhead balcony, completes the home's rear elevation.

A Lifestyle Survey

Here's an exercise. Photocopy the How I Live in My Home worksheet (see opposite page) and the Dream Home Planner worksheet (see page 33), settle down in a quiet spot, and break down a typical week of living. It can be a real week—last week or the week coming up—or it can be an imaginary one made up from the activities done in several weeks' time. Give other family members a vote by having them fill out the worksheet, too.

When they are finished, the two worksheets will reflect how you live, how you use the rooms in your house, and how often. Break down the times of use into mornings, days, evenings, and nights. It may be surprising to find out that many of the hours of the week are spent in just a few rooms out of the eight to ten found in most houses. The worksheets will reveal that some rooms were used the most, some infrequently, and a few perhaps not at all.

LIKES Think carefully about the rooms with the most activity. What appeal do they have? What makes them the center of attention and use? Reflect on how they are configured, how they are lit, and what makes them ideal and functional.

DISLIKES Even though they are used heavily, high-activity rooms still may be less than ideal, and it's just as important to consider the features they lack. Does disrupting traffic flow within or through the rooms? Are they too small or inconvenient? Too noisy? Too dim? The answers to these questions will uncover the aspects that require change.

Then consider the low-use rooms. Were they rooms with no use to begin with, or does your family avoid them because they work so poorly? What causes that to occur?

Top The same space in a home design may express different features depending on personal lifestyle choices. Here, a gabled space is a dedicated home theater. Bottom In another home, the same room becomes flexible and serves for simultaneous TV viewing, music listening, reading, chess, and board games.

Worksheet 1: How I Live in My Home

My home is a:
- ❏ year-round residence
- ❏ vacation home
- ❏ summer/winter home

Number of occupants:
- normal: _____ people
- peak: _____ people

Entertaining

We entertain:
- ❏ frequently (8 times or more per year)
- ❏ infrequently (4–8 times per year)
- ❏ rarely (1-3 times per year)

We entertain:
- formally: _____ X per year   Group size: _____ people
- informally: _____ X per year   Group size: _____ people

Function size:
- ❏ 4 or fewer people
- ❏ 5–10 people
- ❏ 11 or more people

We entertain in our living room:
- ❏ weekly
- ❏ monthly
- ❏ rarely

We dine formally:
- ❏ weekly
- ❏ monthly
- ❏ rarely

Activities

Our activities are usually:
- ❏ individual
- ❏ group
- ❏ mixed

Our activities include:
- ❏ TV/movies
- ❏ card games
- ❏ board games
- ❏ other activities: _____

- ❏ pool/billiards
- ❏ art/photography
- ❏ crafts

- ❏ video games
- ❏ swimming
- ❏ reading

We enjoy activities:
- ❏ indoors
- ❏ outdoors
- ❏ away from home

Most activities are done:
- ❏ weeknights
- ❏ weekdays
- ❏ weekends

We watch movies:
- ❏ once a day
- ❏ once a week
- ❏ once a month

Other Residents

Bedrooms: _____ (number)

Bathrooms:
- _____ private
- _____ shared
- _____ half baths

Residents:
- _____ children full time
- _____ children part time
- _____ elderly adults

- _____ active adults
- _____ visiting guests

Bedroom Needs:
- ❏ homework station
- ❏ detached/handicapped suite
- ❏ private sitting area
- ❏ morning kitchen

Kitchen Profile

We cook:
- ❏ every day
- ❏ 2–4 times weekly
- ❏ once a week or less

We enjoy cooking:
- ❏ definitely
- ❏ sometimes
- ❏ rarely

Our cooking style:
- ❏ gourmet
- ❏ home cooking
- ❏ microwave

We entertain guests in our kitchen:
- ❏ often
- ❏ rarely
- ❏ never

Special needs for our kitchen:
- ❏ double ovens
- ❏ extra refrigeration
- ❏ preparation sink

- ❏ walk-in pantry
- ❏ gas appliances
- ❏ trash compactor

- ❏ eat-in seating
- ❏ wine or beer appliance
- ❏ other: _____

Master Suite Profile

Bedroom: Uses:
- ❏ sleeping
- ❏ reading
- ❏ TV viewing
- ❏ office work

- ❏ desk
- ❏ sitting area
- ❏ morning kitchen

Master Closet:
- ❏ large single
- ❏ his/hers
- ❏ island

- ❏ stackable washer/dryer
- ❏ ironing station
- ❏ mothproof storage

Bathroom:
- ❏ large single
- ❏ his/hers

- ❏ whirlpool tub
- ❏ his/hers vanities

- ❏ adjacent garden
- ❏ makeup/dressing

- ❏ walk-in shower
- ❏ his/hers toilets

- ❏ sauna

Home Office Profile

We use our office as:
- ❏ workplace
- ❏ reception area
- ❏ library
- ❏ retreat

Functions:
- ❏ bill paying
- ❏ computer use
- ❏ file storage
- ❏ faxing/copying

- ❏ reading
- ❏ lounging
- ❏ homework
- ❏ TV viewing

Location with:
- ❏ view
- ❏ seclusion
- ❏ front of house
- ❏ near master

Worksheet 1: Interpreting the Results

The information captured on the **How I Live in My Home Worksheet** *is meant to help the designer and builder evaluate and implement a plan (see prior page). The results will provide useful insights and influence the design process,* *both for the team and you. While there are as many different results as there are families to complete the worksheet, case studies reveal examples of some common yet very different houses that could result:*

Family One: Socially Active

Situation Three family members are full-year residents of the house. At peak times, up to 12 may dwell there during short visits. The family frequently entertains large and small groups, both formally and informally, and participates in numerous activities together. Since the three cooks frequently and often entertain in the kitchen, they want many kitchen extras. They also ask for several extra bedrooms and bathrooms for overnight guests.

Analysis This is a typical profile for a mature professional family with several grown children, each with a spouse and children of their own. A house with large, flexible common rooms and indoor-outdoor connectivity that allows guests to spill out on patios or decks will be more functional and accommodating for varied-size groups. Bedrooms and other private rooms of the house should be situated away from the group activity and entertaining areas. The kitchen should have appliances sufficient for group food preparation.

Family Two: Reserved and Quiet

Situation Two family members are seasonal residents of the house. They rarely entertain but occasionally host intimate groups. Meals are cooked at home two to four times a week, mostly in the microwave. Most of the activities are individual, consisting of watching movies almost nightly, working on hobby projects, or reading. The couple rarely has activities away from home. They ask for a many-featured master suite and a single guest bedroom and bath.

Analysis This is a typical profile for a quiet senior or empty-nester couple. Plan a house with a compact, comfortable family room layout with a home-theater alcove or area, space reducing the kitchen's size. Include a master suite retreat and equip it with a video system, is likely to receive considerable use as a lounge. Provide separate serving areas with wet bars, microwaves, and cabinet refrigerators for snacking and warming take-out meals. Include a combination craft/hobby room. Eliminate extra bedrooms and bathrooms.

Family Three: Full Nest

Situation Two adults and three sports-active children regularly reside in the house. At peak times, as many as ten people occupy the house, and playmates regularly join the family for meals and sleepovers. Entertaining is moderate, mostly for holiday gatherings. Home-cooked meals are prepared daily in an active kitchen with groups coming and going; sit-down meals are infrequent. The family's activities are mixed between group and individual, both inside the house and out.

Analysis This is a typical profile for an active nuclear family. The household needs a home with large, flexible common rooms and indoor-outdoor connectivity, but one that allows change as interests and needs change. A club room in addition to a family room would serve this family well. Casual eat-in seating in a large kitchen, with satellite preparation areas for children's snacks, accommodates the day-to-day meals. A master suite would provide a retreat for parents. Use convertible space for hobbies and to house overnight guests.

Above Giving leisure rooms multi-functionality helps them accommodate both daily activities and occasional light entertaining. This room has a publike atmosphere. It is equipped with a pool table, bar seating, an entertainment center for sports viewing, and appliances for snacks and light meals.

ENTERTAINING Is your household a socially active family that requires ample space to hold a stream of parties, host large gatherings, and entertain guests? How big are those gatherings, and what type of events are they? Do you host formal dinners, more casual buffets and barbecues, or skip entertaining altogether? Is it desirable and practical to have a large dining room you'll use for a holiday family gathering just once or twice a year? Flexible spaces in a smaller and smarter home might better accommodate family, friends, and business entertaining.

OVERNIGHT GUESTS Next, weigh how often visitors stay overnight in the house, especially if they are frequent guests or those with long stays. Accommodating guests means either dedicating space for occasional use or housing them in a room used for multiple purposes. Equipping a room with convertible furnishings or a wall bed is just right for infrequent, short stays, but it could miss the comfort mark for long-duration visits.

Visiting family members might expect to share bathrooms and work themselves into the household, but friends may seek greater privacy. Weigh your needs to decide if it's possible to eliminate an extra guest bedroom and bath in the smaller home's plan. If so, you'll reap major savings, freeing up space for other purposes.

OTHER CONSIDERATIONS Additional factors influence the manner in which you live in your house. In an area with a mild climate, for instance, year-round, indoor-outdoor living can extend your home's interior and functions. Even the house's physical location and the way it sits on its lot might be a consideration. Try to consider factors both inside and outside your house. Is the home set close to the street or farther back? Is your lot narrow with neighbors close at hand, putting privacy at a premium? It might affect how rooms are located or the windows in them are placed. Where are cars parked, and where are the entry doors? Access points to the home may dictate where its kitchen and other rooms are situated.

Left Using built-in and fold-down Murphy beds within a storage wall converts an occasional room to a guest bedroom for visitors. During non-visit periods, the room doubles as a home office, study area, hobby room, or extra entertainment center.

Above A dine-on island for two eliminates the space used by a table with four chairs. The curved countertop extends the eating area but angles the place settings, yielding added space to each side.

Thinking About Size

By this point, you'll have a clear picture emerging of what works in your existing residence along with a good idea of what features and spaces need to be changed. Before jumping ahead to deciding which rooms to make larger, which to reduce in size, and which you might remove entirely, first consider the method you'll use to determine how big to make each room.

When is a room is large enough, comfortable without cramping, or simply wasted space? In essence, how is it possible to "right-size" a house to fit the personal needs of your family and its activities—keeping an eat-in kitchen, for instance, but at the same time making it smaller, smarter and more efficient, too?

SIZE-APPROPRIATE SPACES Right-sizing is just another term for creating a size-appropriate space, adjusting each room to the ideal dimensions that comfortably house its activities. At the heart of planning room size is determining how many people will be using it on a frequent basis and giving it correct human scale. Frequency of use is a key to the first consideration—always avoid setting a room's size based on peak occasional needs—while more practical issues govern the second.

AVOID PRECONCEIVED NOTIONS Many people ask for rooms of a certain size. For example, clients once requested a master bedroom 18 feet (5.5 meters) wide—until they found out their television would be so far away from their bed that they'd have to squint to view it.

It's better to choose room size based on your likely use of it than by matching dimensions to those of rooms you see on TV, in a magazine, or in a model home. Take the bedroom example.

A typical queen-size bed is 80 inches (203 centimeters) long, a dresser is 18 inches (46 centimeters) deep, and a comfortable passageway between them is 42 to 48 inches (107 to 122 centimeters), making the room width 12 to 14 feet (3.7 to 4.3 meters) with a 42-inch (107-centimeter) television for best viewing. Because of the depth of the TV, that saves four to six feet (1.2 to 1.8 meters) of width in the bedroom. Hang a flat-panel TV on the wall, subtract the dresser's depth by locating it to another wall instead of using it as a stand for the TV set, and make the room smaller yet—and shrink the television (and its cost), too.

Use the same logic to squeeze space out of other rooms while retaining all their functionality, even improving their performance. Avoid the wasted space of a kitchen island too wide to reach across, a dining area with proportions different from those of most tables, or entrance foyers deeper than necessary to fully open the front door. Saved space can be put to other uses in the house or help trim its construction budget.

Left Multiple cooks easily share and move past this kitchen's two sinks. The recess of the main sink allows one to work there but keeps the aisle free. A second cook stands at right angles to the first at a prep sink offset 90 degrees; because the cooks aren't back to back, the aisle can be narrow and the room smaller.

BEDROOMS AND BATHS These two important rooms are ripe targets for saving space in a smaller home. In the 1940s, most homes had two bedrooms and a single bath; luxury homes had four bedrooms and two baths. Today, many have five, six, or more bedrooms and nearly as many bathrooms.

At 140 square feet (13 meters^2) for a typical bedroom and 60 square feet (5.6 meters^2) for a minimum bath, these rooms use up to 750 to 900 square feet (70 to 84 meters^2) of space in many homes. If there are enough family members to necessitate them, fine. Otherwise, eliminate or downsize spare bedrooms. Why keep a bed-and-bath suite for use by an occasional visitor? You'll save even more space by switching bathtubs to showers and turning full bathrooms by the family room or laundry into half baths.

Homes with fewer bedrooms and baths once had lower resale values than those of equal size with more such rooms. As baby boomers age, become empty-nesters, and seek to downsize, this is beginning to change. As insurance, reduce the size of the bedrooms rather than eliminate them entirely or make them into flexible rooms that are easily converted back to bedroom use.

Left Individual vanities set on opposing walls in master baths use space better than placing a pair of basins side by side.
Right Freestanding designer-style tubs require less room than those with enclosures and surrounds.
Opposite Incorporating shelving for towels, bars for bath linens, and recessed cabinets everywhere except at the vanity gains extra space for passageways. Using deep soffits beneath the cabinets adds a bit more room where feet tread, as shown here.

OTHER NEEDS INSIDE THE HOUSE Given ideas of how room size is set and where space can be saved, return to examining the rest of the home and its features. Some people say that the only essential rooms of a home are its bedrooms, bathrooms, and kitchen—and while that may be true for minimalists, it hardly applies to a home designed to satisfy its occupants' activities and lifestyle. Other rooms—the so-called occasional rooms—fill the bill when it comes to personalized comfort.

The How I Live in My Home worksheet revealed lifestyle and use patterns. But there are additional considerations in designing

Left Structures sometimes follow the requirements of the site. This steeply sloped lot required building the house into the hillside.

Opposite From within the home, a horizontal beam that anchors the roof to the lower living level becomes a visual element that supports the diagonal windows above it.

a house. Do you have artworks or other collectibles to prominently display? If so, devote a hall or at least a wall to provide space for viewing them. Do you have a special interest or a favorite sport activity you want to reflect? Will your house host special activities such as music performances, dance, or another of the lively arts? Reserve adequate space for these in your plans. Seek out rooms with compatible uses and combine their functions in a single space. In each case, a need will define the details necessary for each use area found within the house.

Wants Versus Needs

About a year after I finished a home for one of my clients, she stopped by my office to let me know how pleased she was with my design. She described the many features of her new home that she used daily, but when I asked her if she was enjoying the new whirlpool jet tub she had me put in her master bath, she just smiled. It turns out the only time she had ever filled that luxurious tub with water was to wash her dog.

———————

The cardinal tests used to separate wants from true needs are practicality—the "Will I really use it?" question—and budget impact. Now that you have a list of needs and wants, it's time to set priorities.

Do you need a special space for certain activities—a quiet spot for a child's homework, for instance? Do you require a home

Fitting a Home to Its Neighborhood

Only part of your smaller home's design deals with its floor plan and interior. In truth, these will be shared only with your family and close friends. The exterior of the house, by contrast, will be marked by its suitability and compatibility with its surroundings, and everyone who passes by will view it from the street.

In this era of tract homes marked by a few repetitious designs that look nearly the same, matching a home to its site occurs rarely except in custom developments. Still, a replacement home or a remodel built into a row of Arts and Crafts, Georgian, Queen Anne Victorian, or Spanish ranch homes must be compatible with them if it is to to achieve its full potential. To make the match, the design must repeat visual architectural details of and borrow color schemes from its neighboring structures in the community. Elements such as rooflines, exterior finishes, columns, and window treatments complete the integration.

Beyond the design details, the way the home functions in its setting also affects compatibility. Setbacks, yard widths, entry walks, landscaping, and other elements are key to blending a new home with the existing structures found in its surrounding neighborhood.

Above This kitchen includes a number of features that tailor it to an active family with diverse schedules. The island provides seating for informal breakfasts eaten on the fly. The kitchen table is a place to eat meals together. A secretary station adjacent to the counter is used for bill paying or searching online for recipes and shopping. A triangular area allows cooking to occur out of the flow of traffic to the stairs and other rooms, yet the cook remains connected with other family members.

Opposite Making useful space for hobbies that require limited space such as crocheting or quilting are best accomplished by locating them in corners or nooks rather than by creating larger, dedicated rooms for a single purpose.

office? Do you have an elderly parent living with you who requires a ground-floor suite? Pay close attention to these real needs.

Your leisure activities and hobbies should be part of the plan, too. Are your evening hours filled with conversation and games, or are they spent lounging in front of the television? Will space be needed for crafts, sewing, or the like? Do you spend your time reading, or would that overstuffed chair in a sitting area's corner in the master bedroom just be a magnet for dirty laundry? Is the enjoyment of cooking sufficient to warrant a gourmet kitchen, or will take-out meals heated in the microwave be the rule? Should an area be set aside for formal dining, or are evening meals quick family-at-the-kitchen-counter events? Always question whether your home's rooms will be used as expected.

Once you have developed a priority list based on proven needs and established desires, use your budget to tailor the house to fit.

Sharing a home office means accommodating each occupant's interests and activities.

Above top A desk used for e-mails, research, or calls usually still has some available surfaces for decor.

Above bottom A home office might need unique solutions to keep the work area free of clutter. Use wall shelves and hangers to store items for occasional use or to personalize the space.

Above right The wife's workspace reflects her more feminine nature and the needs of her business. Her space also has chairs for reading or an occasional visitor.

Budgeting

The informal priority list is valuable as a starting point to define a new smaller and smarter home. To test it, set an affordable budget for building and outfitting the house. This is when you'll weigh priorities on the scale of available resources.

Make a ballpark estimate of the amount of square footage in the home you want—a rough range is OK—based on your guesses of the number and sizes of its rooms, adding a bit for wall thicknesses, other needs, and just for safety. Write down all the assumptions, or use a computer spreadsheet to keep track of your thoughts. Next, place calls to several local residential builders and design firms. Describe the home's expected size and features, and ask the experts their typical per-square-foot (per-meter^2) costs for building similar homes in the area, including their fees, the land, and likely upgrades. With experienced firms, guideline construction estimates that closely agree with one another are likely (if not, see When Bids Differ, opposite page).

Left The husband's desk is located across the room from his wife's (see opposite page) and reflects his sporting interests through wall decor. It has ample space for handling a nightly load of paperwork and the laptop he brings home with him from his day office.

Multiply your estimate of square footage by the highest of these estimates. This number will yield only an empty house on a bare lot and, while it's important, is only the beginning since you'll refine it during the design process. The actual budget for designing and building a house includes everything required to outfit it: paving, wallpaper, painting, window treatments, furnishings, and land-scaping, even swimming pools and shade covers. These items can add 20 to 30 percent—or even more—to the land and construction budget. A budget is all-inclusive to the point of being move-in ready.

Depending on your expectations and priorities, the rough budget will range from acceptable to sobering; it may be shocking and require a step back. If the initial figure you calculate is too high, even by just a bit, turn again to the priority list. Estimate the cost of each extra listed as a want rather than a need, weighing its personal value against its expense. Scrutinize all the must-haves carefully, minimizing their space use and features. Pinch, squeeze, and trim any fat to arrive at a final budget for the house and all its trimmings.

When Bids Differ

It's tempting to dream about getting a great deal on building a new home—using the friend of a friend to save half or more of its construction cost—but bids that seem too low most likely are. They may result from omissions, errors, or outright fraud, but it's certain they lack something essential, from quality materials or skilled labor to liability protection insurance, performance bonds, or payroll taxes.

Scrutinize low bids carefully, asking questions about how bidders determined their numbers. Ask them how they are able to achieve lower costs than other reputable competitors in the area. Their answers may be unsettling and informative.

It's also fair to question a bid that is higher than the others. The answer might reveal an item or two that were left out of the lower ones. Avoid a hard fall by being realistic and certain that all costs are covered.

Providing a snack and beverage area in the corner of a family or club room is a wise choice for an active family. Such features limit the traffic flow to and from the home's kitchen and are good places to eliminate clutter with out-of-sight storage.

Remodeling Versus New Construction

While both construction processes have common factors, remodeling projects are remarkable because of the degree to which they add stress to their owners' lives and disrupt homes, making them unlivable for long periods of time. In remodeling, power or water may be disconnected, and noise, dust, and tradesmen become near-constant companions.

Another difference is demolition. Unlike the methods shown on popular television shows, removing cabinets and flooring, tearing out walls, and exposing plumbing and wiring takes time and care. Waste and debris must be disposed of safely. New construction begins only after demolition ends.

Many times, plans must be revised when unexpected conditions are discovered: termites, rot, settling, sagging beams, cracked foundations, out-of-square walls, and the like.

All of these factors mean that remodeling jobs can be expected to cost more and take longer than their equivalent in new construction.

Organizing a Program

The process provided here gives much insight about where and how living takes place in your current house, plus understanding of how a new or remodeled smaller and smarter residence could provide still-higher quality and enrich your life. Only now, with the priority list of wants and needs, space requirements, and budget estimate in hand, is it possible to specify the details of the new home you want.

COMPLETE THE PRIORITY LIST Review the wants list for opportunities to save space and money. There may be items that slipped past the earlier screenings. On a recent project, for instance, I had a client who originally wanted a walk-behind wet bar but chose a more space-efficient wall bar instead.

Make a new enlarged photocopy of the My Dream Home Planner worksheet (see opposite page) and complete it. Detail information for each room of the house. Flag items that are still wishes rather than requirements, and note any upgrades. Each important feature you require should be noted on the worksheet.

Worksheet 2: My Dream Home Planner

Rooms of a Smaller and Smarter Home

	EXAMPLE (Kitchen)	Kitchen	Leisure room	Master bedroom	Master bath	Formal living room	Formal dining room	Bedroom 2	Bedroom 3	Bathroom 2	Bathroom 3	Nook	Study	Laundry	Office
Is this an essential room?*	10														
How often will the room be used?†	22														
How strongly is the room desired?*	10														
Can uses be com-bined in the room?*	8														
PRIORITY RANK (sum of prior rows)	**50**														
Use 1	Cook														
Use 2	Eat														
Other uses	Party Pay bills														
People (normal occupancy)	2														
People (peak occupancy)	10														
Desired features	Island Pantry Hood 2 ovens														
Flooring	Stone														
Wall finish	Paint Tile														

* Signify importance by entering a number between 1 and 10 (1 being least important, 5 being neutral, and 10 being most important).
† Enter a number equal to the number of times the room will be used in a typical week.

Interpreting the Results

The worksheet compares each room's importance, expected uses, and features. Entries made to the first four rows add to a single priority measure for each room. (Two individuals might weigh entries in the first, third, and fourth rows differently on a ten-point scale, but each will use the same scale to compare rooms in their own house). If the example kitchen—50 priority points—is compared to a formal dining room with scores of 5 for being essential, 1 for times of use, 8 for desirability, and 10 for combination potential (a total of 24 points), the kitchen is highest in priority. Other rows capture items designers need to plan each room.

Left and opposite The renovated San Francisco urban dwelling seen here and on the opposite page was first built in 1906 as temporary housing for victims of the historic earthquake and fire, but it has been occupied continuously for the past 100 years. It fills a narrow strip lot with minimum setbacks on three sides and shares a common wall with its neighbor on the fourth. At 2,200 square feet (204 meters^2) it has a spacious living room, kitchen, and dining room on its main floor, and a master bedroom suite, office, and garage beneath. Rooms on the main level share two decks that permit indoor-outdoor living in the city's mild climate. Natural wood floors and wainscoting with open-gable ceilings add to the expansive feel of the bungalow.

ASSEMBLE A TEAM Building a new house—or remodeling an existing one—is a team effort. Because your vested interest in the outcome will affect the quality of your house, choose wisely each of the consultants who will help plan every detail of the home's design and the construction project.

The team will consist of an architect/designer, an interior designer, a general contractor, and a landscape designer. Start with the firms that earlier provided construction cost estimates (see Budgeting, page 30) and expand the vendor list by identifying and interviewing local members of the National Association of Home Builders (NAHB) and visiting model homes. View the Web sites of the American Institute of Architects (AIA), the American Institute of Building Design (AIBD), the American Society of Interior Design (ASID), and the American Society of Landscape Architects (ASLA) to find local member firms to round out the team.

Shop around, using the same criteria as you did for the preliminary budget. As before, avoid automatically going with the lowest bid and consider tossing out any bids that are way outside the pack, whether higher or lower. Try to isolate why bids differ to make sure that each bidder is estimating the same job and that nothing is overlooked. Assemble the entire team at the onset of the project, when the My Dream Home Planner worksheet is complete and firm (see page 33). Each specialist will contribute valuable ideas to the project, and the group will work together to create a cohesive plan that makes the most of the priority list and any other objectives.

Be honest with the team. There's a prevailing thought that keeping the actual budget secret is smart because the team's members would spend it all if they know the total. That's false. In the end, when the secret, true budget is revealed and plans must be scrapped, time and effort will have been wasted. Professionals will respect a fixed budget, even strive to beat it, and they'll spend less and work better than they would if they were kept in the dark.

BUDGET, SCHEDULE, AND SPECIFICATIONS With the design and building team in place, outline the final budget and detailed specifications for the house and reach consensus on a completion schedule. The professionals' years of experience will be an invaluable asset to you as they "value engineer"—save money on—the home's rooms and features and help steer the design toward solutions they've learned over many jobs, avoiding errors and oversights.

With the team's assistance, your dream of a smaller home will eventually become building plans, specification lists, materials, and labor.

The goal at this stage is to achieve a realistic budget and a set of specifications on which the entire team will focus its energy. Take the time to explore options, add back elements that were

reluctantly sacrificed during the trade-offs to achieve cost savings, and modify thoughts about the house's look and feel. This is your opportunity to have a smaller home, one customized and personal, one that is simultaneously comfortable and unique.

DESIGNING THE SMARTER HOUSE So far, this has been an inner journey that has explored your current life habits, how those habits might change in the future, and the act of paring down to the essentials which of those needs and wants should be memorialized in timber, glass, concrete, and stone.

The goal is to have a new residence that is smarter and more comfortable than your current one. Whether your objective is to downsize, move from an apartment to a first home, or realize the dream of a forever-after house, it leads to a path unique to you and different from those followed when other homes in your neighborhood were built—one less focused on size and more on quality and comfort—with a resulting house that mirrors that quest.

The principles that govern the design of a smaller home are applicable to structures of any scope, shape, design, or scale. Livability is paramount in a well-designed house, and waste is a foreign concept within its walls. Instead of grand spaces that seem cold and unwelcoming, seek quality in workmanship and fine finishes. Rather than seldom-used rooms that make up a showcase, aim for a home that mirrors your personality, activities, and lifestyle.

Now is the time to prepare for the magic to come: designing, sketching, saving space, combining or eliminating rooms, and creating functional and interactive spaces to uniquely fit you.

Opposite left A sloped two-acre (0.8-hectare) lot had plenty of space to accommodate a large, northern California mountain retreat, but the owners sought a small-scale home that better fit their lifestyle and habits. The result was this home of 2,700 square feet (250 meters^2).
Opposite right and below left A loft over the great room shares space for a guest bedroom and a home office. The French doors maintain privacy and quiet sound while giving these rooms views through the expansive windows.

Below right Using a space-saving corner tub in the master bath on the home's main floor gives the room a treetop perspective yet maintains perfect privacy on the secluded site. The sloping lot makes the room sufficiently high above ground level to place its windows in the forest canopy.

Go with the Flow: Space Planning

An open-plan, smaller home requires a smarter flow than a house divided into many single-purpose rooms, yet it still must comprise ample size, convenience, and beauty. Those goals are key to the next steps in space-use planning. Strive for an optimum layout containing these three important categories of spaces:

- Interactive spaces
- Multifunctional rooms
- Combined indoor/outdoor spaces

Spaces that interact with one another echo principles, themes, and designs drawn from classic structures. Instead of dividing your interior spaces with walls, allow functional areas to flow seamlessly within the house, even passing right through its outer walls. These spaces will be more welcoming and have improved traffic flow. Move a step closer to conserving space and gaining convenience by combining several uses within each room. Rather than setting aside space for a single function or purpose, give your home the many benefits of unified spaces—most notably, convenience and conserved space. If you live in a temperate climate zone—most of the United States—expand the living areas of the house by integrating outdoor-use areas with adjacent interior functions.

Opposite A multifunctional, eat-in kitchen with both counter seating and a separate table is situated on the main level of a home of 2,500 square feet (232 meters²) located in Seattle, Washington, seen here and on the following two pages.

Above left The three levels of the home are served by a tensioned steel-and-wood stairway. The home's stairs and corridors have exceptional traffic flow capacity.

Above right Rectangular motifs repeat in the room's shape, arched openings, and kitchen island. Light and dark finishes contrast with light wooden cabinets and furniture, allowing hue precession and recession to amplify its depth.

Why do these design principles of the smaller home seem revolutionary? The paradigm of a house as a collection of single-purpose rooms stems from societal custom and experience. This thinking implies that any house with new functions must grow in size and have a new room added for each feature it gains. How did this common though mistaken belief arise?

Fundamental lifestyle changes, dating from the 19th century, led to the one-use, one-room principle of space planning. During the Victorian era, visitors were formally entertained in entry foyers and front parlors while only close family and friends freely entered the rest of the house. Dining rooms were intermediate spaces shared by visitors and family alike. Physical barriers—walls and closed doors—masked the home's occupants from prying eyes, but they also isolated family members from one another.

In the years between 1971 and 2005, as lifestyle changes repeatedly added new activities and functions, following this trend meant increasing the size of the average house in the United States by more than half, reaching an average of 2,340 square feet (217 meters^2). And the trend hasn't abated: more than half of all houses built today are larger still.

Remodelers of older residences sometimes reflect on this historical change when they find it necessary to tear out walls to enlarge kitchens, add bathrooms, or make other modernizing changes. Rather than divide a family, a house should be a refuge for its members and should help to bring them together.

Today's largely informal lifestyles dispense with many reasons to automatically choose space-wasting, single-purpose rooms. Homes are better suited to open and interactive floor plans.

Left High ceilings overhead and a roof overhang shelter the second-story great room and its deck with views of Lake Washington. Using tall rooms within smaller spaces creates a sense of volume.

Above top The lowest of the home's three levels house a garage and two bedrooms. The second story contains both cooking and living areas, while a third floor holds the master suite.

Above bottom The house sits on a dimensioned concrete block plinth to maintain its scale, and its design suits nearby traditional neighboring homes.

Left **This transitional remodel of a contemporary-style home uses neutral color schemes to create gallerylike spaces suited to the owners's growing photography collection and contrast with its antique furnishings. The brick fireplace was reconfigured to a clean, flush-to-wall form with rectangular proportions similar to the nearby window openings.**

Opposite top **Light spilling onto the open-beam ceiling creates strong diagonal lines to accentuate the room's dimensions and space. Rectangles of furniture and walls in different shades of gray provide the room greater depth.**

Opposite bottom **While the home features an open, L-shaped plan surrounding its central fireplace, it has well-defined boundaries for the dining, living, and sitting areas.**

Interactive Spaces

Creating zones of activity within free-flowing, open areas that our senses interpret as spacious rather than confined makes a smaller, smarter home possible. Using interior detailing to denote boundaries—instead of raising walls—creates use areas within the space of an open plan. Rooms become interactive, multi-functional, and inviting. Edges are marked by arches, columns, borders, material transitions, and distinctive ceiling and floor treatments. Pocket doors provide privacy where it is required, but in essence the soul of the smaller home is its open functionality.

Open space gains flexibility that is impossible through the traditional division of rooms by doorways, halls, and walls. Each time a single, unified area replaces several smaller rooms, a sense of spaciousness is born that better reflects modern lifestyles.

Most families are studies in division and perform various tasks simultaneously—from a commuting father or mother watching the morning traffic report and kids grabbing a toaster treat before heading to school, to trying to wash the laundry in a utility room filled with crafts projects or sports gear. Recognize this multi-tasking reality by making the home more efficient, restoring space for group activities, and promoting shared participation even when your family's members are engaged in separate activities.

SPACE-SAVING ROOMS Spaces become interactive when the walls that divide them are removed. Whether the intent is to create a space to replace a kitchen/nook/dining room/leisure area or to plan a master bedroom suite/bath/walk-in closet/lounging area, removing corridors and barriers opens up vistas within the house, makes the resulting room more inviting, and encourages the family to interact. It's also easier for several family members to cooperate in a single area with divided usage than it is for them to compete for space in a single-purpose room.

Each wall that is removed from a house means space saved. When walls are taken out, the corridors needed for traffic to flow within them and around furnishings are discarded, as are hallways that formerly joined rooms together. The result is a more efficient use of the remaining square footage (meters^2) in an area that feels more spacious. As a design principle, combining rooms into interactive spaces yields a smaller and smarter home.

More Hall

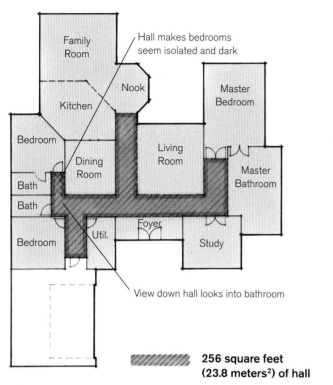

Hall makes bedrooms seem isolated and dark

Family Room

Nook

Master Bedroom

Kitchen

Bedroom

Living Room

Dining Room

Bath

Master Bathroom

Bath

Foyer

Bedroom

Util.

Study

View down hall looks into bathroom

256 square feet
(23.8 meters²) of hall

Less Hall

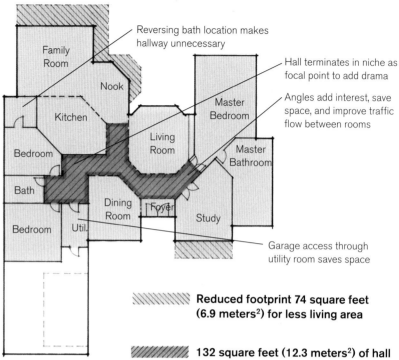

Reversing bath location makes hallway unnecessary

Hall terminates in niche as focal point to add drama

Family Room

Nook

Angles add interest, save space, and improve traffic flow between rooms

Master Bedroom

Kitchen

Bedroom

Living Room

Master Bathroom

Bath

Dining Room

Foyer

Bedroom

Util.

Study

Garage access through utility room saves space

Reduced footprint 74 square feet
(6.9 meters²) for less living area

132 square feet (12.3 meters²) of hall

Above left Poor traffic flow results when rooms are isolated from one another and reachable only through hallways or by passing through other rooms.

Above right Removing walls but defining corridors with distinctive flooring treatments links areas within the home, reduces the distance traveled between the rooms, and increases the feeling of connection between them. Area devoted to halls and the footprint of the house is reduced.

INTERACTIVE EFFICIENCY Sharing space is generally more efficient than traditional room division because it joins and overlaps use areas. Soft, flexible boundaries permit groups to expand or shrink use areas, in either expected or unplanned ways, as they need more or less space for their activities.

An entire family can share an interactive space even though their individual activities and pastimes may be diverse and primarily solitary. An open-plan family room easily accommodates several people at the same time, some of them watching television or playing a video game as others study, write, read, listen to music, sew, or play board games. Members of one group join another, and the space shifts to make room for them. In planning each room, make sure that your family's activities won't compete with one another for the same space, causing conflicts.

Interactive rooms suit many areas of a home—they even expand to the outdoors with window walls, French or sliding doors, or flexible partitions that allow living areas to spill onto nearby decks, patios, or verandas. A kitchen-leisure area, for example, may open to an outdoor dining room and barbecue area, a screened porch, a swimming pool, or other transitional space while a bedroom suite may include an adjacent courtyard or balcony. Indoor-outdoor interaction during the warm seasons of the year means a smaller footprint for your house while retaining the space characteristics of a much larger structure.

If your home is to be made up of a cluster of open, interactive rooms, examine how each of these spaces is reached from the others, how space within it is defined, how those spaces work internally, and whether it satisfies the needs of the whole family.

Left Replacing walls and doors with broader openings and giving rooms multiple entry points adds to their sense of spaciousness.
Right top Wall segments joining and between rooms keep spaces separate and provide opportunities for architectural details and features such as this fireplace.
Right bottom Furniture clusters also help define the boundaries and use areas within a room.

Above left Changes of levels serve to divide open space as well as other design techniques. In this home, built on a sloping site, the living room is at the same level as the main entry. The remainder of the house's main public area is a few steps down.

Above right Open diagonal views from corner to corner and from the lower dining room to the upper living room add to the apparent space of the open plan. Though both rooms are joined, they interact with one another as though they were wholly separate.

CREATING INTERACTIVE SPACE A smaller area results when two rooms are reconfigured into one. In the case shown on the opposite page, traditional formal dining and living rooms waste space. In modern smaller homes, retaining the usefulness of these separate spaces must weigh against practical use and budget issues. The option shown here combines the two into an equally ample yet smaller configuration.

Removing the wall between the two rooms makes it possible to eliminate the wall's width and the corridor space between the parson's and dining tables, a net gain of four feet (1.2 meters) over the separate-room option. A group deep in discussion at the dining table can share the room with others conversing on the sofa, yet still enjoy their separate conversations. The real bonus is that the room feels larger joined than separate. To help delineate two spaces such as these, vary the room width at the junction and use distinctive ceiling or trim treatments for each area.

Another reason to use interactive space in this manner is the greater flexibility the final room has for furniture placement. Consult your team's interior designer to gain the greatest space savings and the most attractive finished result.

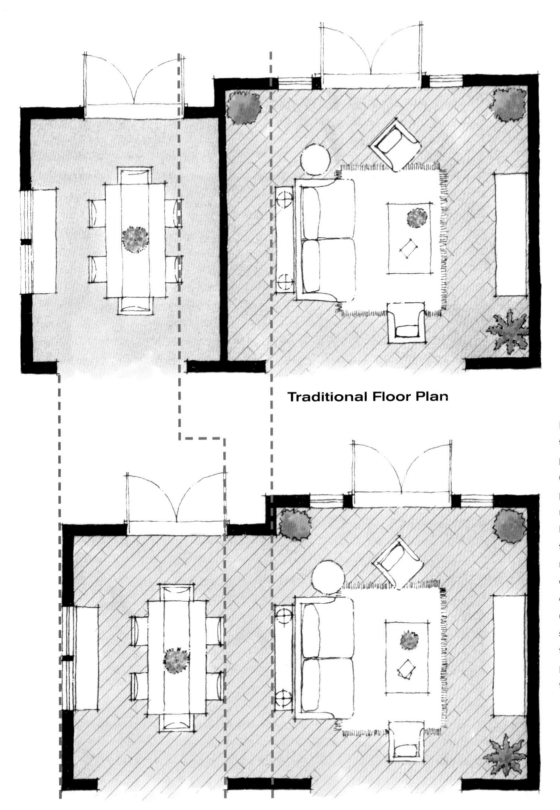

Traditional Floor Plan

Open Floor Plan

Before and after. You'll see this typical living room/dining room pairing in many traditional homes (top). Dividing two rooms with a permanent wall requires an allotment of space for passageways between the wall and each room's furnishings. The length of the room is narrowed by the width of one corridor and the wall itself once the dividing wall is removed (bottom). Besides benefiting from space savings, the interactive room feels larger than the traditional pair did and has more options for furniture placement.

DOUBLE-DUTY THINKING The principles of designing inter-active spaces can be applied throughout your house, but there are some practical limits to open-room design. Privacy issues, tendency toward clutter, and other personal factors restrict interactivity. Adolescent children need private space, for instance—and, from time to time, so do their parents. Laundry rooms, utility rooms, under-stair closets, basements, and attics require new approaches to achieve their full potential in terms of interactivity. In some cases, it may be better to keep separate rooms but plan for combined uses.

You could use a single room as a playroom and guest room, incorporating a fold-down Murphy bed for overnight visitors or merge a library or den with a home office. In both cases, the uses mesh well without clashing. By contrast, mixing a guest bedroom and a home office in a single space might make for an uneasy fit if you have to work to do while a visiting relative wants to sleep in the room.

Another place where double-duty thinking makes a difference is in a stairwell. You could save 18 to 24 square feet (1.7 to 2.2 meters^2) by using a single run stairway over a double run with a

landing, but consider instead enlisting the space on landings for a home office, study nook, or storage area. Build cabinets under the stairs, make it into specialty rooms such as wine cellars and darkrooms, or reclaim its overhead wall space for shelving and hanging garments. With quality design, such spaces are attractive, efficient answers to real needs for functionality while still avoiding the use of dedicated rooms.

A short passageway between a kitchen and dining room is an ideal spot to tuck in a butler's pantry, sink, wine storage appliance, and bar, eliminating the space needed in the dining room for a sideboard. It's an out-of-sight spot to refill glasses and place dirty dishes, helping to keep the dining table and kitchen counters and tables clear of clutter.

With quality design, double-duty spaces provide attractive, efficient solutions without taking up the space of dedicated rooms. Just as important as the principles that go into designing them is an understanding of how traffic flow patterns—both within and between rooms—affect a house's open design.

Left **Stairways and their landings are good places to look for space-saving inspirations. Rather than focusing on their roles as ways to connect floors, use them as niches to provide additional functional space such as this homework station.**
Above top **Recessed, built-in shelves are a natural for use beneath runs of stairs.**
Above bottom **A threshold step to the study's level helps divide the workspace from the stairs.**
Opposite **The perch area over the stairs becomes a reading nook with natural light and great views through the great room's windows.**

Above Using diagonal elements when dividing rooms eliminates visual cues drawn from corners to make rooms feel larger and helps improve traffic flow. This sitting area backs against a kitchen.

Right Angled curves of the kitchen counter follow the dividing wall. A pass-through allows clear sight lines across the room's center.

Opposite Using a diagonal in the kitchen opens triangles of floor into separate workstations, helping it to be more efficient.

HEAD OFF HEAVY TRAFFIC Every house has choke points, places where doors, halls, stairs, or furnishings combine to block aisles or otherwise make it a challenge for people to pass and stand comfortably. Interactive rooms lessen the number and severity of these roadblocks, but you'll also save space you eliminate these situations from a smaller home:

- Access to a room through another room or hall
- Aisles blocked with furniture
- Counters or tables with chairs protruding into walkways
- Exterior entries passing through multiple rooms
- Interior portals sized to fit large appliances and furniture

Some rooms will naturally gather groups. Trying to cook dinner in a kitchen filled with numerous family members or guests—even helpful ones—is easier if the kitchen features extra corridor space, has workstations to accommodate the overload, or uses an angled layout to expand its workstations and traffic areas.

To avoid traffic bottlenecks, include in your kitchen plan several access points for each use area. Use partition walls and cutouts so communication and passing plates are possible without the need for a physical passage. Eliminate choke points at doorways by replacing traditional doors with a wide arch or a pair of columns. These define a room entry just as well as doors while keeping the corridor open. If you prefer the privacy a door offers, opt for a pocket door. Because it requires no swing, it saves space and improves traffic flow.

Family rooms are another gathering point; provide sufficient space for furnishings and group movement. Give them nooks for game tables and snack centers.

Note all the entry points of the home—doors near parking or sidewalks—and place destination rooms close to them. Bathrooms near entries from your yard, for instance, stop muddy trips through kitchens or family rooms. For doors from attached garages, allow sufficient width to let kids run past as you carry groceries in.

Right **In the soul of every laundry and utility room lurks the potential for a family studio—a hobby room and laundry combined with multi-functionality. All it takes is a few more square feet (meters^2) of area.**

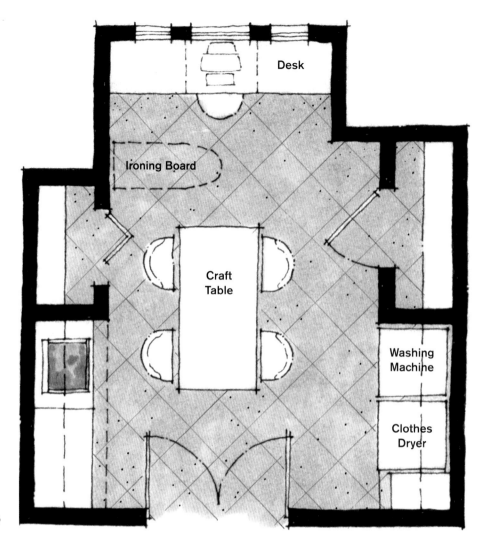

Desk

Ironing Board

Craft Table

Washing Machine

Clothes Dryer

Family Studio

Multifunctional Rooms

At its heart, every interactive room in the smarter house is also multifunctional, combining the uses of two or more individual rooms within a single conjoined space. The house gains some function by combining rooms specifically to work together in this fashion, but it saves even more space by allowing most of its important single-function rooms to pull double duty. Here are some examples:

A FAMILY STUDIO An example is the typical laundry room: for the most part it's hidden, stark, utilitarian, and dedicated to the weekly wash. The illustration above shows that, by expanding a room from 50 to 90 square feet (4.6 to 8.4 meters^2) in size, the laundry transforms into a crafts room, linen closet, pantry, home office, and bill-paying station. It is outfitted with a whirlpool-jetted utility sink to launder delicates, a washer/dryer pair, an ironing station, closets for clothes and staples, a home computer, and a table, desk, and chair.

Whether having an expanded room such as this means that closets, home offices, or other spaces can be eliminated from your house is a choice driven by their final ranking on your priority list. Certainly, however, the multifunctional laundry room has the potential to make your smaller home even more efficient. The pertinent question is whether family members would be more likely to spend time for the same activities in this family studio than they would in other parts of the home.

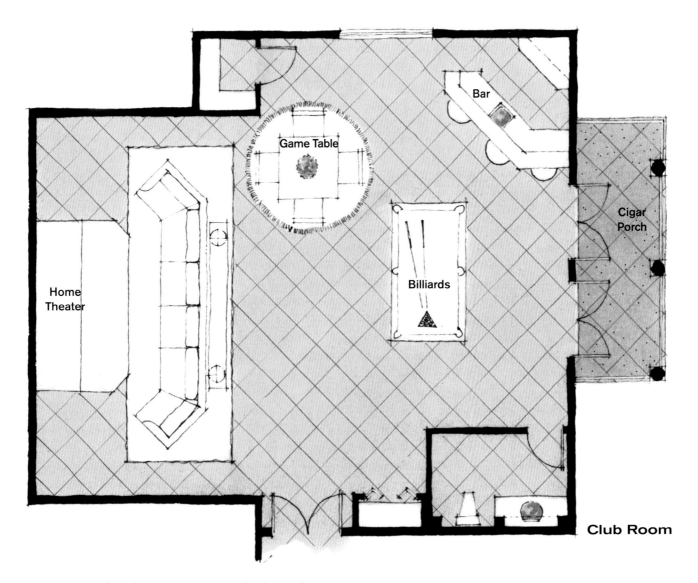

Bar

Game Table

Home Theater

Billiards

Cigar Porch

Club Room

A CLUB ROOM If you're like many people these days, you might prefer one room with a single, dedicated purpose—a home theater, for instance. Ask yourself how often your family will use such a space and whether you would be better served by a club room, such as the one illustrated above. This multifunctional room includes the theater; places to play board games, cards, and billiards; a bar for snacks and drinks; a cigar porch; plus a half bath and ample storage for music, games, videos, and electronics.

Can you envision your family at leisure in such a club room—together, actively involved yet enjoying individual pursuits? It's a highly functional use of an area of 300 to 480 square feet (28 to 45 meters²) that substitutes for several single-purpose rooms.

Above In the same fashion as the family studio replaces a traditional utility room, a club room is a great room or family room on steroids. It should be customized to serve all of a family's activities, making it a core for the house.

A LEISURE ROOM One of the most promising areas of a home for multitasking is the leisure or family room. As a priority item, these rooms always rank near the top of the list. They have the most demands placed on them: watching television, listening to music, socializing with family members, entertaining friends, eating informal meals, appreciating views through their windows, even snuggling up to a cozy fireplace—all in a single place. By default, a leisure room is a space defined by and for multifunctional use.

Because flexibility is already inherent in a leisure room, it may deserve to stand alone. Make it interactive with other parts of your smarter home by using arched openings or columns to define its boundaries, granting easy access to the kitchen, dining area, and nearby patios and decks of your house. Allow for a full spectrum of future changes—new babies or family members leaving the nest, redecorating, involvement in fresh activities and pursuits, additions to art or literature collections, and other transitions—so that the room remains adaptable over the lifetime of the house.

A KITCHEN When does a home's main food preparation room become more than the standard kitchen? Give it a butler's pantry, a wine cellar, an eating and conversation area—with window seats, counter bar, table, or a booth—or allow its doors and windows to open freely to the yard, pool, courtyard, deck, or patio. Dividing the space into use areas means that crowds become groups, work is shared, meals are more lively and enjoyable, and after-dinner conversation lingers.

Top **A diagonal bedroom corner rarely serves real needs. It is an ideal spot for a fireplace.**
Bottom **Setting doorways and arched openings out from a corner makes useful alcoves for furniture without impeding traffic.**

Opposite **When the space for an alley-style kitchen is narrow, open it up to the adjoining room with an arch and a counter. Both rooms' interactivity is improved because a serving area was included in the pass-through opening.**

A MASTER-BEDROOM SUITE The typical master suite is like a studio apartment, with a bedroom, vanities, bathing areas, a private toilet, and a closet—each a single-purpose room. Try instead a semi-open plan using back-to-back or divided vanities, a walk-in shower, and built-in cabinets for clothes, towels, and linens—but keep the water closet private, either as a single or a pair. Complete the multifunctional room with an open passage to the bedroom containing a sitting area or window bench.

Your household's size, your way of entertaining, and your lifestyle will influence your choices of features to combine or keep separate in every space.

Above left Specialized lighting fixtures make alcoves more inviting by drawing attention to displays and furniture within them.

Above right Arranging wall sconces and art in a linear pattern in recessed niches on stairways at the same slope as the stairs helps break the repeated horizontal lines of adjacent rooms.

Planning Ahead

Hidden behind your house's walls, or in its closets, attic, or basement, are systems for plumbing, electrical, and heating, ventilation, and air-conditioning (HVAC), plus specialty controls such as media, cable or satellite television, data, security, telephone, wiring for doorbells and thermostats, even ductwork for whole-house vacuums. Some systems are compact and have a single purpose; others are bulky and multifunctional with planning requirements. Both types are worth researching before you make final decisions for locating them in the house.

Rely on your design team's advice to evaluate your priority list, recommend equipment, and find a place for it in the house. Here's helpful information worth considering:

PLUMBING Locating plumbing fixtures and pipes adjacent to a common wall—called a "water wall"—thick enough to contain the diameter of waste drain and vent pipes, reduces the amount of plumbing materials needed and the cost of installing them. The economies of water walls for showers, tubs, toilets, sinks,

Left The needs for electricity, plumbing, and natural gas lines for an island are planned in the design stage. Large kitchen appliances such as ranges, ovens, and cooktops require their own heavy-duty circuits.

dishwashers, washers, refrigerators, and faucets usually means bathrooms, kitchens, and utility rooms are positioned back-to-back or atop one another in multistory homes.

Rural houses get water from wells and drain their waste and sewage to septic systems. Urban and suburban homes are connected to municipal water and sewage systems. Plan for instant water heaters to meet household needs, plus a water-conditioning or reverse-osmosis purification system in hard-water areas.

FURNACES AND AIR CONDITIONERS Furnaces and dual heating/cooling units such as heat pumps are heavy, bulky pieces of equipment that require indoor space for installation. Oil and propane furnaces need fuel storage tanks, while natural gas heaters are plumbed with gas lines. Air conditioners have indoor heat exchangers and outdoor compressor/fan units connected with insulated refrigerant and condensate lines routed through walls, floors, or ceilings. An important factor for all HVAC equipment is proper sizing. Consult a qualified specialist when planning HVAC installation.

ELECTRICAL SYSTEMS Household electrical systems include electrical and electronic wiring, telephone and TV cable wiring, and specialty wiring for computer networks, security and alarm systems, doorbells, media, and household appliance controls.

Advances in automatic lighting control systems make a world of difference in the use and efficiency of modern homes (see Whole-House Technology, page 130). Preset dimmers control individual fixtures and banks of lights to set levels suited to the way the room is used—full illumination for task lighting and less for mood. Sensor switches turn lights on and off as they note your presence or when doors open and close. Automatic control systems adjust each room's lighting to the time of day, note when night falls, and tailor illumination needs as programmed.

Use Modular Construction

Ask the team to standardize dimensions to common modular lengths if possible. Using modular components and standard windows saves costs over custom ones. Standard-length frame members eliminate waste and time, saving labor and materials.

Above Belying its 1,600 square feet (149 meters²), this Methow Valley, Washington, cabin has a glass box of flush-set windows anchored by a structural frame of massive beams.

Opposite Hinged double doors and window walls make the deck of a Seattle home–also shown on pages 64 to 67–a seasonal adjunct to the living room.

Inside Out

Walls of windows are another useful element in making your smaller home feel larger than its actual square footage. Thanks to the remarkable development of windows with insulating properties, you can have visually open spaces without sacrificing energy efficiency.

Each window is really two or more panes of high-technology-engineered glass mounted in an insulated frame with inert gas sealed between them. By reflecting infrared heat rays, these dual-pane windows retain warmth indoors or block exterior heat. They

have the added benefits of reducing glare and screening ultraviolet rays that cause furnishings to fade.

Glass gives nearly limitless opportunities for opening up interior spaces of your smaller home. One of the most effective strategies is to place windows and glass doors on opposite walls in the corners of a room. This removes the visual cues that define the edges of the room, creating a vista of the outdoors and the feeling of unlimited space. Use the technique for second-floor bedrooms, leisure rooms, and kitchens, wherever adjacent outdoor areas provide on-demand extended space.

If you live in a warm climate, make seasonal use of the outdoors an integral part of your plan—this strategy is useful even in temperate climates, now that materials exist to limit heat loss and gain. Where practical, bring the actual outdoors to your interactive spaces with movable glass partitions. Sliding back a window wall to incorporate an outdoor porch dining area or a swimming pool deck means that functional areas within interior rooms flow freely into their outdoor counterparts. Add more insulation to low-E, or energy-conserving, glass walls when it is needed with exterior shutters, awnings, and manual or automatic window coverings.

FLEXIBLE SPACE You might be tempted to create permanent spaces in your home for infrequent events such as large parties and holiday family gatherings that happen just once or twice a year. A better solution is to include on-demand space for these functions. When space uses multiply, it helps a house flex.

Exterior balconies, porches, courtyards, and decks are good candidates for convertible spaces that become part of the house's interior; provide access with sliding glass doors concealed in the walls. For a more traditional look, opt for double French doors or build a window wall four feet (1.2 meters) outside the house's main walls and join it to the structure with partitions on each side containing entry doors. Enclosed courtyards give privacy within houses for spas, fountains, or water gardens; for use across the seasons, equip them with sliding-glass doors and a vented skylight.

Inside the house itself, plan flexible rooms with areas within them to handle overflow crowds from the family room, dining room, or kitchen. A cojoined leisure room or a library, for instance, might have features to welcome additional diners or be a spot to set a buffet table or bar instead of using the main eating area.

Consider the placement of rooms and how they connect when planning flexible spaces in your smaller and smarter home. Open floor plans work best when their visual sight lines along corner diagonals remain unobstructed as they pass through multiple rooms. These vistas are important to making the home feel spacious. Create open sight lines by using arches rather than doorways, aligning aisles and corridors in a series, incorporating pass-throughs and portals in solid walls, and placing walls at angles to the rooms.

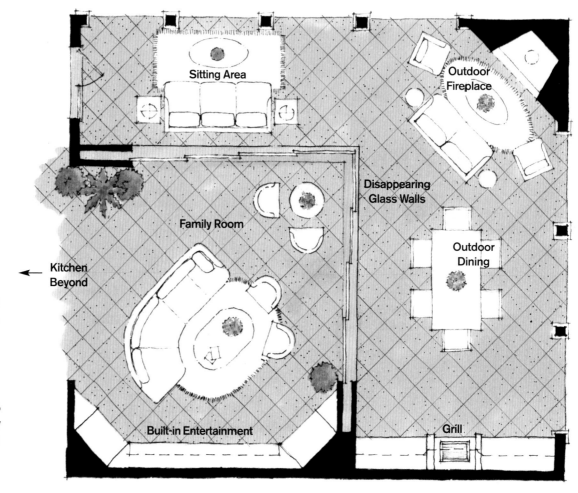

Right Indoor and outdoor spaces merge in a room with walls made of disappearing glass. When the weather is inviting, they recess into pockets, opening the room to include adjacent porch areas. When inclement conditions occur, they close and become completely weathertight, yet retain the visual openness deemed essential in a smaller home.

Interior and Exterior Flexibility

Open sight lines between floors are another planning consideration. Position upper-floor rooms behind an interior balcony or staircase with a setback from the railing to give them privacy even as they remain interactive with the rooms below. Use pocket doors, sliding panels, French doors, and curtains as temporary dividers when necessary.

Above This room executes the same concepts shown in the illustration on the opposite page. Here, a kitchen and its adjacent sunporch are unified in a flexible indoor-outdoor space.

OUTDOOR LIVING SPACES Another effective way to expand the livable space of your home is to include outdoor sunrooms or sunporches—called "solanas" in tribute to their Latin American heritage. Focus a solana on a single feature such as a fireplace or include an area that serves as a dining room, outdoor kitchen, or cabana. A solana can be built on the ground or as a balcony, deck, or suspended porch.

Enhanced yard and garden areas, used during parties and gatherings as overflow spaces along with a home's interior, may become your favorite parts of the house. These spaces give the home dramatic accents and enormous flexibility, and they also enhance its value while replacing floor space in the structure itself.

How do all these elements function in actual structures? You'll see most of them in the project that follows on pages 64 to 69.

Left Top Walled garden patios become extensions of the rooms within the house, adding to their appeal and enjoyment.

Left Bottom Simple barbeque areas are transitioning to outdoor kitchens and lounging areas in many areas where year-round outdoor living is the lifestyle.

Opposite Situating sunrooms, courtyards, and even pools near bedrooms, dining rooms, family rooms, and kitchens provides seasonal living areas without encumbering the main structure.

Euclid Residence

Seattle, Washington. Balance Associates Architects

This contemporary 2,500-square-foot (232-meter^2) residence is home to a professional couple. Built on a sloping site adjacent to an urban wilderness park, it affords great views east to Lake Washington, the city of Bellevue, and beyond to the Cascades.

In order to minimize its tall, narrow appearance, the house is broken into three visual units: a base, two central sections, and a floating cap. The splayed base anchors the home to its hillside setting amid soft greenery trained onto trellises. The second unit comprises two boxlike forms containing the main living area and separated by a flexible vertical circulation space with expansive glass and 12-foot (3.7-meter) ceilings that give the space a loft-like feel. A broadly overhanging pair of gable roofs make the final unit of the structure, capping its form, mimicking the distant mountain range, and paying homage to—and providing protection from—Seattle's famous rains. Walls of glass set in a structural frame give the illusion that the roof hovers overhead.

Although the flexible living space is enclosed by glass, the house is very energy-efficient. All of its windows face south or east to take advantage of the light and warmth of the sun. The high-performance glazing limits heat loss, and the rest of the building is heavily insulated. Infrared and humidity sensors control the house's passive ventilation system, a necessary function for this tightly sealed structure.

The home is an innovative design solution to a small-footprint lot with unstable soils, incorporating many interactive spaces, multi-functional rooms, and connectivity to the outdoors.

High Definition:
Interior Detailing

At my firm, we strive to create four-dimensional architecture. Home designs may address the aspects of space planning and elevation style, but rarely do they bring that style past the front facade to its other elevations, and more rarely still to the home's interior. Too many houses are beautiful architectural shells with stripped interiors that miss out on matching the coordinated details of their exteriors with the spaces inside— the places where people actually spend most of their time.

You have established the priorities, needs, and wants for your smaller home and have considered where to place them in its context. Your creative team will work out the details of a floor plan that is within budget. It's time now to focus attention on the home's interior details. Trim, finishes, and other detailing shape the house's character and clearly define its use areas.

Think first in terms of definition. Details of worksmanship and choices of materials convey impressions both visually and tactilely. If the room is your canvas when it comes time to create definition, detailing is the paints and brushes you will use to achieve these effects.

Which elements create depth, color, edges, and textures? How will shadow and light help? Begin exploring your options by understanding the rules of proportion.

Opposite **A wealth of detailing is evident in this home's rooms. From the fine moldings on its columns and chair rails to the space-defining changes in its ceiling and flooring treatments, each individual decision helps to build the room's character. Additional views of two houses built to this plan are seen on the cover and on pages 70 to 73.**

Above left A barrel-vaulted corridor separates a compact kitchen from its adjoining dining room. Proportions make each room an extension of the other. **Above right** To the front of the house, a casual great room shares the kitchen with eat-in counters. **Opposite** The great room offers panoramic views of the water near Savannah, Georgia.

A Sense of Proportion

I once had a client who insisted on a ceiling out of scale with the room's size. Despite my pleadings, he was convinced that the greater the height, the grander and more impressive the space. He wanted to convey substance but instead only demonstrated capacity—the room affectionately came to be called "the silo." It lacked the proper proportions necessary for a room of its size.

Before outfitting rooms with crown moldings, finely detailed columns, or other features, look at their proportions. The rooms' size relationships affect what feels comfortable in them and influence what details to use.

Ancient Greeks developed golden-mean proportions based on their mathematical observations of nature and applied those proportions to their architecture. Asian cultures judged proportions by the circle and used it to create many distinctive structures. Either standard yields rooms with pleasing proportions that adapt well to their furnishings. Think in three dimensions, evaluating the relative size of the room's walls compared to its floor and ceiling.

Use detailing to divide a room that feels too long and narrow into two or more sections, each with more gracious and pleasing proportions. Restore proportion between its sections and define space in the room with changes of ceiling, floor, or wall materials. Use arches, columns, corners, indents, windows, or trims to mark transition points between the room's functional areas.

Square rooms convey stability through regular proportions which are consistent with formal themes. If your goal is more casual, interrupt their repetitive geometry with organic elements such as angled walls, curves, or irregular shapes.

You can also use visual illusions to establish perspective. The mass of light-colored ceilings and their apparent distances from observers seem greater than those with dark hues. You can achieve similar effects with carpeting, tile, and wood floors. Selectively lighting one area instead of another brings emphasis and division to the space. Even faux-paint techniques such as the realistic perspective landscape wall murals employed in trompe l'oeil styles—three-dimensional illusions to deceive the eye—serve to alter a room's sense of space and perspective.

Above **Upstairs, a master suite bedroom opens to a traditional railed balcony with vistas. Every part of the house conveys a sense of comfort and spaciousness.**

Opposite top **A shady porch with square stucco columns repeats the upper floor's theme for the main living area of the house. This flexible space is freely accessible from inside the house.**

Opposite bottom **The front of the house has many dimensional levels unified by their repeating roofline elements.**

Wulfert Point

Sanibel Island, Florida. Sater Design Group

This modern update of a 2,873-square-foot (267-meter^2) Charleston Row home (seen here) has detailing with many Bermudian and Bahamian influences. Its banded and detailed stucco exterior walls are mirrored by faux-painted plaster walls indoors. Radiating panes accent the circle-head windows that repeat throughout. The same plan built in Savannah, Georgia, offers an alternate vision (see cover, page 9, and pages 68 to 71).

Interactive rooms on both levels of the two-story home open to outdoor rooms with saltillo pavers replacing wood flooring and pairs of double French doors to mark the transition. The doorways

frame exterior views of subtropical foliage and, from the second story, vistas of Sanibel Island. Within the home, crown moldings in gloss enamel stand in relief to the brightly colored, sponge-finished walls, providing contrast in both color and texture.

The interior of the home is a reflection of its exterior style and treatment. Choices of railing treatments, transitions from square to tapered round columns, and trimmed ceilings add substance and perspective to the structure.

The home is a close contemporary fit with its neighbors, reflecting a rich heritage of communities that once filled the island. Built on a shallow lot, the house utilizes the private side courtyards as flexible space for relaxing and entertaining.

Left and opposite The views on these two pages are from different rooms of the same house. The bathroom at left picks up a color scheme complementary to that of the kitchen. Carrying a single color palette throughout the home expresses a warm ambience made even richer here by using sponged paint. The use of detailing becomes most evident when the designer singles out a feature to showcase such as the glass basin in the bathroom resting on a stone slab with its surround of limestone tile or the distinctive kitchen hood shown on the opposite page. Such elements draw the eye and, together with the color scheme, establish a mood carried by decor to the entire house.

Inside and Out

Your smaller home's design and architectural style will give essential clues for the detail palette from which to choose its interior finishing touches and decor. The rooms of a house fulfill the promise of its exterior motif, and the front door of a home built in French Country style that opens to rough-hewn stone, rustic beams, deep window sills, and earthy tones will be totally consistent with its curbside promise.

Repeating specific exterior details inside unify the house. Among the features of a home's exterior worth repeating indoors are these:

- Columns and ceiling treatments
- Arches and beams
- Repeating surfaces and patterns such as stone and brick
- Door and window-frame detailing

Above **The living and dining rooms of this narrow-lot home share unique ceiling treatments and built-in cabinetry. Their four pairs of French doors give access to a wide veranda.**

Reprising these exterior elements of your home lends continuity and familiarity throughout its structure, enhancing the whole.

Lend credence to your home's style and reflect its geographic region's heritage by choosing community- and climate-appropriate paint and trim schemes in its interior detailing. Dark wood floors add richness to traditional homes located in well-established suburbs, but they might feel discordant in a modern-minimalist house in a city. If your region is filled with sunlight, a tropical color palette of airy Caribbean-themed hues, the white-and-earth tones common to the pueblo region of the Southwest desert, or the rose-and-cream shades of the Mediterranean are similarly appropriate when they are used within the context of the house's design style and material choices.

Capture these prevailing regional traits with themes based on historical precedent—coastal charm, Victorian opulence, or colonial cozy—in such signature feature details as a window of stained glass or painted filigree railings.

Another place to reflect exterior architecture is in the choice of materials. Wrought iron and dark, rough-sawn wood are equally appropriate elements for a Tuscan home, an adobe ranch, or a Spanish mission-style house, as are carefully turned spindles, honed and polished rails, and pickled wood floors in a Pennsylvania Dutch farmhouse or a Cape Cod bungalow. Each detail helps complete the house's personality.

Stamp individual spirit on your home's details to make it personal, but rely on the design team's experience to suggest appropriate interior details and finishes. The advice of professionals is especially important for choices of columns, stairs, and doors, because these highly visible and distinctive features speak directly to the interior's compatibility with the home's exterior.

Left Note how the two rooms work together to define a common space and theme. Shared details make this possible, from the divided windows over the doors and the running bond of hardwood strip flooring that spans and unites the entire length of the space, to the columns and arch that divide it.

Mood and Character

Matching details, materials, and finishes to each room's purpose are important for setting the room's mood and giving character to the home. Detailing choices reflect both the function and the ambience of the room and carry to those of a home's other spaces.

Create an atmosphere that reflects purpose by keying off how rooms are used. Formal moods for areas such as living rooms mean using coffered ceilings and rich crown moldings, while casual rooms such as club or leisure spaces might have rough-sawn beams and natural-finished, tongue-and-groove wood ceilings.

ADDED DETAIL LENDS CHARACTER Too often, houses have interiors that are barren of detail. Each layer of character is cumulative, so note the progressive change as you add each new element. Start with a practical matter by choosing flooring materials or coverings suited to the intended use. Tile may be the right choice for a bath, laundry, or entry, but may be unsuitable for a bedroom or study. Plank or parquet wood belongs in a hall, den, or home office, and wall-to-wall carpeting provides comfort and warmth for casual and semiformal areas of a home. Other options include brick, stone, and linoleum—even cork.

Consider next the wall textures and color scheme of the house. Instead of knock-down and spatter-textured wallboard, use skim-coated plaster, smooth or rough finishes, or paint effects such as ragging, rolling, and sponging to enhance character, build depth, and add texture through color rather than surface. Use of field colors that contrast with nearby trim elements adds visual depth and apparent texture. Murals with trompe l'oeil effects are the last word in creating faux depth on flat walls.

Left **If you frequently hold dinner parties, placing a dining room in an area off of an entry foyer eliminates the need to include a seldom-used living room in your home's plan. The dining room achieves this by featuring elements usually seen in a living room such as the quality detailing in ceiling, windows, and floors demonstrated here. Devote the space saved to other areas such as club rooms, great rooms, or family rooms.**

Opposite **For families used to having more casual meals, color and furnishings establish mood when a room's features and style support the effort. Here, under-stated crown moldings and window trims are the background for a strong color scheme and arresting decorator touches, making for a playful and fun overall effect.**

Right While traditional coffered ceilings run parallel to the walls, setting them in diagonal galleries emphasizes the room's breadth and width. Alcove shelving beneath an arch make the complementary curved desk of this office a centerpiece of attention.

Opposite left The same alcove concept applied to a bathroom makes a whirlpool tub inviting. Here, the window's arch repeats the form of the barrel-vaulted ceiling and the curve of the tub.

Opposite right Rustic beams and wrought iron bring a Southwest mood as their intersecting lines shorten the depth of a long hall by arresting the eye's travel.

CEILINGS Turn attention overhead to the ceiling's height and its finish. Using taller ceilings is important in a smaller home. Ceiling heights greater than the eight feet (244 centimeters) used in most homes add volume to rooms. They make possible the use of varied-height cabinetry to increase interest and provide additional storage capacity, and they offer opportunities for moldings and other details that would be lost on lower ceilings.

The most economical optional ceiling heights—subject to the rules of proportion—are nine feet, four inches (284 centimeters); ten feet (305 centimeters); and 12 feet (366 centimeters), because they are standard measurements for drywall, lumber, and other sheet building materials, allowing for waste-free construction.

Besides height, you have other choices when it comes to ceiling construction and finishing. Some popular ceiling styles include:

- Vault: with pitches to a slope. There are barrel and pyramid vaults, along with groin vaults with intersecting vaulted arches.
- Gambrel: two parts, shallow slope above and steep below.
- Tray: shaped with an indented surface, with either sloped or stepped sides.
- Coffer: recessed panels defined by intersecting beams in either square or diagonal, gridlike patterns.
- Cove: similar to a tray, featuring recessed shelves that hold indirect lighting fixtures.

Left Room detailing portrays either formal or casual moods. The playful outcome in this lounging room devoted to music depends on the rich color treatment of the ceiling, along with irregular placement of the musician cutouts and furniture. **Opposite** By contrast, a very formal statement results from careful combinations of symmetry in the presentation of elements, selection of colors, and use of classical arches with a faux-painted groin ceiling.

OTHER CONTRIBUTIONS TO MOOD Ceilings, walls, and floors are enhanced by moldings that add character and detail to their forms. Choose crown moldings and finely chiseled base-boards to add transitions to a room's corners, or apply wainscoting and chair rails to lend depth and richness to its wall surfaces.

Fine woodworking also plays a contributing role here. Carefully turned handrails on stairs, carved doors or lintels, built-in shelves, fireplace mantels, and cabinets faced with veneer or inlay—all are examples of craftmanship used to enhance the mood of the rooms in which they are installed.

You'll add to the character of a room with detail headers over doors and arches, soffits in ceilings around the perimeter, and moldings on corners. Every element you add contributes to the overall effect of a room, working together to define its mood.

Right Teens' bedrooms and guest rooms are good candidates for saving space by replacing traditional closets and chests of drawers with sitting areas, built-ins and niches.

Opposite Rustic shelves recessed into the walls are equally suitable for storing books or displaying collectible items. These units free up floor space when compared to freestanding shelves. Collecting and aging wine was a hobby of this homeowner. He installed a temperature-controlled wine cellar that stores 600 bottles of fine wine in a corner of this basement room.

NICHES AND BUILT-INS Use alcoves in the end walls that terminate halls or are adjacent to entry doors, place niches along stairways, and include built-ins throughout the home as functional and visual elements to add interior mood.

Alcoves are floor-to-ceiling recesses used to showcase tall sculptures, house a bench, or frame other furniture. Treat the interior surfaces of an alcove differently than the surrounding wall to make the alcove feel deeper and more distinctive than it otherwise would.

Niches serve as more than display shelves for art and collectibles. They create recessed focal points of interest in the wall, allowing three planes of display: framed art hanging on the wall, the wall surface itself, and the niche.

Built-ins are essential in the smaller home to replace storage in freestanding bookcases, armoires, buffets, chests, cabinets, and other pieces of furniture. Include them in or adjacent to your home's walls to increase the usability of perimeter space. Expand the depth of key interior walls and column details to allow construction of built-in shelves, cabinets, and niches that break the plane of the wall and add space-saving, off-floor storage. Also plan to include built-in window seats with storage drawers beneath or a lid that opens.

WINDOWS AND DOORS It's a common practice in architecture to orient the structure to the site in ways that place its windows and doors where they will feature the site's prominent views. Consider also where each door and window can be used in such a way that it improves a room's interior appearance, enhances the traffic flow of the house, or affects the furniture placement within it.

Window walls help a house's interior communicate with the outdoors, and they flood the interior of a home with natural light. Use them in rooms that will be used primarily in the morning or evening. Place them on sun-facing exposures only if you live in a high-altitude, cold-winter region; if you live in a warmer climate, shelter large windows under an overhanging roof to avoid excessive midday heat gain.

Glass doors, windows, and window walls are excellent for bringing north light into an otherwise shady side of a house, but privacy can become an issue on some sites. If your home is situated too close to neighboring houses, use windows high on the wall instead. While ensuring privacy, high placement also increases the sense of volume in a room because the directional light from above fosters a perception that there is open sky beyond the windows.

A window can be its own architectural statement—as in the case of a large circular port on the midpoint of a stair landing or a focal point created in stained glass. In multiples, windows can form groups. Place windows in arrays of three or five, two patterns that are visually pleasing. A large central arch with two side arches repeats classical themes, while a tall, narrow window in the center with two smaller flanking windows to each side creates a geometric pattern that fits ideally in the space under the vault of a gabled ceiling.

Doors—whether single, double, sliding, French, or Dutch—help set the mood of each room. Use doors with either single or divided panes of glass to help convert closed passages into inviting, open halls. Choose doors with ornate carvings and inlaid wood to create an entirely different feel.

Decide whether doors will remain open in interactive convertible spaces, will be opened as needed to accommodate needs while entertaining, or will remain mostly closed.

Left Making a design statement by choosing unique windows and doors establishes a theme for the residence that begins with its main entry.

Opposite top This contemporary-style house is located in Marin County, California. Its corner windows on both levels levels are key to making the main interior rooms of the home feel spacious and open.

Opposite bottom Visitors preview featured elements of the home's interior through the glass entry facade. For its owners, the facade opens views from within the house and from its cantilevered stairway to the nearby water, islands, and sky.

Left Using arch pairs creates an attractive frame for features seen through the openings much like the effect achieved by matting around a painting or photograph. **Opposite** An arch with paired edge soffits has a pleasing geometric form when it is used in combination with a barrel-vaulted hall ceiling.

ARCHES A series of rectangular or curved arches help divide rooms, galleries, or halls, adding definition and depth to their long dimensions and helping to create pleasing visual planes of light and dark. Construct arches with jointed moldings, frame them as integral parts of the wall, or support them with free-standing columns. To add interest to a rectangular arch, consider using stepped or curved corners at the transition points where the arch's sides meet its header. If the arch is curved, barrel-vault the room or hall's ceiling at the same radius or add extra detail with intersecting groins extending perpendicular to the barrel vault to mimic the arch's form.

Mount lights to accentuate or illuminate arched openings, install windows that extend from the floor to above eye level in the walls of the hall, or plan cutouts in the wall to frame views into other interior rooms. The patterns from the lighting fixtures, windows, or cutouts create illusions of depth along the length of the hall and add spaciousness and appeal. Indirect lighting fixtures in coves or downlights in a ceiling achieve the same effect.

Above Whether indoors or out, the combination of a welcoming fireplace is the focus of attention in this inviting room. Such key features should be planned to make optimal use of the room and set the space's theme.

Opposite Striking panoramic views from the Oakland hills to San Francisco Bay dominate this room's exterior view. Placing the minimalist fireplace at the wall's centerpoint with its metal and maple-panel surround gives a visual reference point to anchor and provide contrast with the scenic grandeur.

Taking Center Stage

Decades ago, builders in our area discovered plant shelves. At first, they were nearly magical elements used in moderation for adding interesting accents between the glass doors and the transoms above. Soon, most new homes sported many such shelves, which in turn fostered a booming silk-plant business. The shelves quickly became common, overused, then cliché. I learned my lesson. Now I am careful to use such features in moderation—abundance makes them ineffective.

Architectural elements of a room go a long way to establishing its proportions, character, and mood, but the icing on the cake are featured elements that catch the eye and focus attention.

In each major room of your smaller home, weigh options for a feature to act as a centerpiece. Examples include fireplaces, hoods, entertainment centers, bars, library walls, specialty bathtubs, and novelty sinks, among other choices.

Think about how the feature affects the room's proportions, and give it prominence by centering it on a wall, placing it in a corner, allowing it to protrude into the room, or by locating it in a lighted alcove where it will draw attention. Next, consider the effect it will have on the room's character and mood as you choose from various model styles and colors. Here's another opportunity to draw on the house's architectural style, whether traditional, rustic, casual, formal, or contemporary. The featured element can match, contrast, or harmonize with other elements and treatments.

A dry-stacked, natural-stone fireplace, for instance, is fitting for a rugged yet refined mountain home, while a hand-carved limestone fireplace surround might be the ticket for either a sophisticated French urban dwelling or a Tuscan-themed villa seeking to evoke a mood of the 17th century.

Whichever fits the house's style, carry the theme through-out the entire home. A carved-stone kitchen cooktop hood, for example, might fit in better with cut-stone tile backsplashes, pottery sinks, and enamel cooking appliances than does one made of stainless steel. Choosing it for use in the kitchen makes it likely that similar features and materials would be worth repeating in other rooms of your house.

————————

Defining and detailing your home will make it graceful and elegant. Keeping clutter to a minimum is another essential element of planning its design and requires next a discussion of storage.

Above Matching an architectural feature to its setting develops the context of the room. The style and subdued colors of this cut-stone fireplace are a good foil to the neutral hues of the room's walls and furnishings.

Opposite Developing contrast–using enamel-white moldings and stone tiles for this fireplace's mantels and surround–bring it to the forefront and help it dominate the rich yellow walls.

Right Strong colors dominate the living spaces of the house. From the details of its architectural design to its vibrant warm colors, every aspect of the house evokes happiness and fun.

Opposite A group of three arched and divided-pane windows caps the sidelight windows and lower doorway of the great room. The residents and visitors may choose to enjoy as a focal point either the room's central fireplace or the tree-lined views outside.

Santa Rosa

Rehoboth Beach, Delaware. Sater Design Group

Snug yet spacious at 1,978 square feet (184 meters²), this three-bedroom Key West home was transported to the Delaware shore, yet it retains aesthetic aspects of its Caribbean heritage.

Requiring a footprint just 42 by 48 feet (12.8 by 14.6 meters), the house has a central great room rising from the entry stairs with a signature fireplace, a window wall, and a vaulted ceiling that soars to the second floor and beyond. The room opens through sliding doors to the rear porch. This central gathering place joins the home's main living and cooking quarters, leaving the upper level for a master bedroom suite. Repeating elements with bows and curves—the balcony rails, window tops, and columns—contrast with the uniform rectangular geometry and proportions found in the rest of the house. Strong use of color predominates, another conch touchstone to the Florida Keys.

The kitchen ceiling is a tray design, defined by broadly curved crown moldings. In contrast to the shiny stainless steel appliances, extra tall, dark-wood cabinets with diminutive pulls float from the walls, echoing the dark strip wooden floor underfoot.

Materials for the finish features of the home were carefully chosen to lend richness and texture yet avoid detracting from the simplicity of the design, from the ceramic tiles selected to surround the master tub to the round-bullnosed granite of the sinuous kitchen counters. The divided-light windows are made of multi-pane glass surrounding integral moldings, and they are carefully finished with wooden frames and sills. Perhaps most notable are the richly colored strip-plank wood floors used throughout.

Out of Sight

Over the years, clients have requested many special closets. I've been asked to design closets to hold baseball memorabilia, doll collections, wrapping paper, fishing lures, even one for an assembled Christmas tree (decorations and all). I even had one client who loved her clothes so much that she wanted a bed in her walk-in so she could recharge herself after an extended period of viewing and selection.

Planning adequate storage space can be a challenge, but a closer look at the issue of storage often revolves around proper utilization rather than the actual quantities of closets you need.

When thinking about storage, keep in mind that linear footage and organization matter more than area, and that walk-in closets, however spacious, require proper design in order to yield the most efficient storage space compared to other closet options.

While space left over after room allocation is commonly used for storage, planning for it from the beginning is a better choice. Your storage needs are as important a consideration as any other space in your home. Think beyond the traditional closet layout: Concealed built-in cabinets, efficient organization systems, and maximized vertical storage in taller cabinets are all options. Look critically at seemingly unusable areas as opportunities for storage.

Opposite Built-in wardrobes, cabinets, and in-wall or under-bed drawers eliminate the need for freestanding furniture and save space while providing ample storage for clothing and personal possessions. The daybed rests on a full-depth drawer cabinet that holds linens. The overall effect is spacious and tidy.

Right Hidden storage, whether built into the house or a late addition through its furnishings, makes double duty of space. Ottomans and coffee tables frequently contain drawers, racks, and shelves for storage.

Planning structural storage into your home at the design stage means that it works with the home's furnishings to provide the flexible storage a family needs, grant easy access to possessions, and avoid the appearance of clutter.

Using storage built-ins is a convenient way to divide your belongings and place frequently used items near points of use instead of combining them in large groups stored in out-of-the-way spots and used only occasionally. Built-in chests, armoires, entertainment centers, buffets, servers, wet bars, and bookshelves are just a few options available to you as places in which to store linens, clothes, utensils, appliances, electronics, and more.

Traditional freestanding furniture sits within the room where it eats into the room's floorspace and places limitations on its design possibilities. By contrast, integrated built-ins adapt to any space or use need you envision as you build your house.

An important advance in storage solutions came with the introduction of built-in, structured closet systems. They include nearly ingenious organizer and cabinetry units configured to use nearly every bit of space and adapt to most needs. Depending on their purpose, they revolve, unfold, extend, and retract, making spaces for useful storage that otherwise would be lost.

Planning structural storage as an integral part of a smaller home involves another room-by-room evaluation that relies on your design team's experience. Tell them clearly what you require, and the designers will provide specific, efficient solutions to accomplish your goals.

Left Turning passageways into storage areas such as this butler's pantry uses minimal space in the overall plan, but it places usable cabinets and drawers near prime locations where they are needed. It stores occasionally used dishes and utensils in a convenient, yet limited-access spot.

Above Ingenious built-in cutting boards and drawer systems maximize the space of cabinets near a range or cooktop.

Above right (clockwise from top left) Cabinets with appliance lifts solve the problem of storing and accessing heavy utensils and their many accessories. Dual-sided-and-hinged shelves make the interiors of overhead pantry cabinets conveniently accessible. Narrow slots between lower cabinets are ideal locations to hang a supply of dish linen. Open baskets on sliding extender make good room-temperature storage locations for root vegetables that require ventilation.

Eliminate Kitchen Clutter

Factory-engineered and assembled cabinets make possible unparalleled quality and features; most are economically priced. When planning kitchen storage using these preassembled cabinets, keep these options in mind:

- Increasing the height of countertops and cabinet depth adds storage capacity and ergonomic benefits to a kitchen design.
- Extending the height of upper cabinets to the ceiling provides extra storage for seldom-used items.
- Using space-framed cabinetry and flush-mounted hardware when possible permits full use of cabinet depth.
- Concealing frequently used appliances such as toasters, coffeemakers, and mixers in an appliance garage located on the counter backsplash between the upper and base cabinets allows for easy access while keeping counters free of clutter.

- Considering cabinet configurations that avoid units with excess depth, hard-to-reach corners, and inaccessible voids.
- Utilizing innovative hardware such as lazy Susans, pullout trays, and dual-sided shelves to provide easy access to the entire depth of each cabinet.
- Installing drawers and bins with organizers or panel separators rather than using cabinets with shelves helps group loose objects out of sight.
- Adding under-upper cabinet storage bins and drawers provides space and organization for such items as recipe cards, staples, clipped coupons, and the like.
- Placing concealed slide-out drawers to hold pans and cookie sheets in the toe-kick areas beneath the cabinets and in fillers between main runs of cabinets takes advantage of these otherwise wasted spaces.

Above Temporarily expand work space by drawing a table out from its cabinet nest, then pushing it back in when the need is over.
Above left Using bins to store staples, citrus, and vegetables helps to give a country kitchen a vintage atmosphere. The frosted-glass frames make it easy to see what's inside each bin.

Above top An appliance garage for countertop appliances hides clutter yet retains easy availability.
Above bottom Stacked baskets pull completely out of their nesting cubbies so access to their contents on the countertop is easy.
Right Cabinet doors with shelves use the full depth of the recess, while under-cabinet drawers file recipes in a place convenient to where food is prepared.

Opposite left Multitiered pantry cabinets feature folding, double-sided shelf units in front of fixed shelving, all concealed behind doors fitted for additional storage.
Opposite right (from top) Corner carousels serve storage from areas previously lost. Shallow drawers concealed behind cabinet doors are good for storing flat placemats, linens, and other items. Pot drawers under a cooktop keep utensils and pans close at hand for cooking.

Preassembled cabinets are only one choice; there are also custom and semi-custom cabinets. In every case, solid-wood cabinets are more durable than those made of pressed wood composite board, and they are more easily refaced with new veneer and doors a few years down the road when you want to remodel. If you're likely to change the entire kitchen layout during a remodel, however, select the most economical cabinetry possible with good finish detailing, since it will probably be kept in service only five to seven years.

With well-planned special storage cabinets in the kitchen, a separate food pantry may become unnecessary.

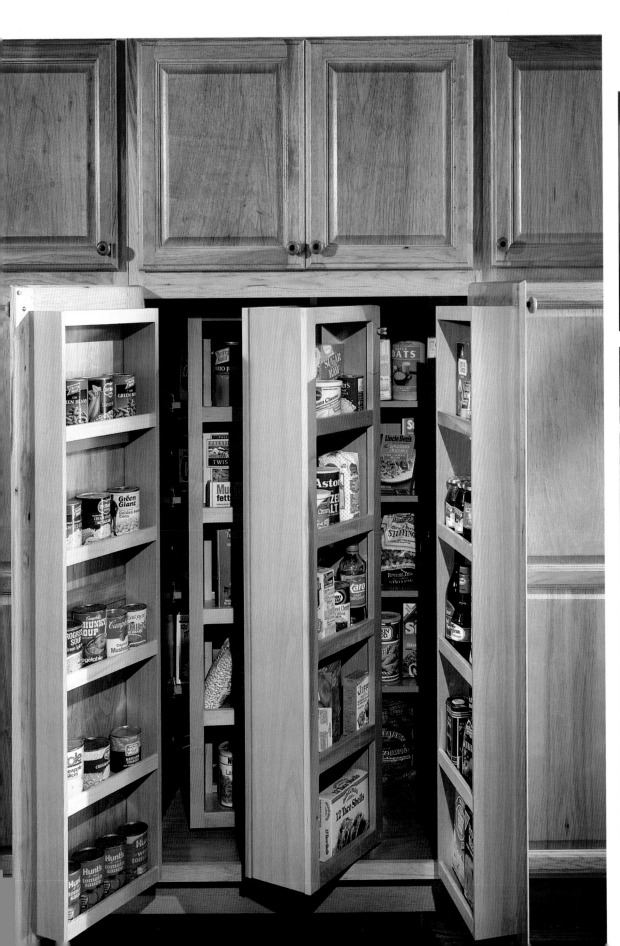

Tidy Laundry and Hobby Areas

Enhance service and utility areas of your home by providing a combination of built-ins or other flexible storage cabinets, ample work surfaces, and counters.

If the house design permits, consider overhead storage in the attic space over the laundry room with access through a pull-down extendable ladder. If you plan to add structural storage in the attic, advise your designers so they can make allowances for the added load. In a home with a basement, provide easy access to it from the utility room or garage.

Increase cabinet storage capacity in the room and reduce back strain by increasing the height of countertops. Extend overhead cabinets outward a few inches (centimeters) as well. Mount free-standing and in-cabinet shelving on adjustable tracks for maximum

flexibility in storing both short and tall supplies such as laundry detergent and spray bottles. Add a flexible cabinet on casters that can be stowed in an under-counter bay but can be moved anywhere it's needed in the room.

Outfit upper cabinets beside the dryer with extending pull-out rods to hang laundered clothing and a storage bay for laundry baskets. For easy garment repairs and touchups, consider a built-in desk with drawers to hold a sewing machine and a garment steamer. Install a built-in wall cabinet containing an iron, ironing board, and aerosol cans; the board pulls down for use and stows behind the cabinet door in seconds.

Include at least one full-height wall cabinet with an upper shelf to hold mops, brooms, vacuums, and other tall items. If you have young children, provide a locking cabinet for hazardous storage.

Family hobby and fix-it supplies—tools, glue guns, adhesives, hardware, gardening tools for houseplants, and other items—can be organized in drawers and cabinets customized for that purpose. This means including both deep and shallow drawers and bins, flexible cabinet shelving, and wall organizers. Ask your design team to specify under-cabinet lighting fixtures to illuminate work surfaces and provide ample power outlets for tools on the walls, both at work counters and along the floor.

If the laundry room also serves as an entry from the garage or other outer door, stop boots, raincoats, and umbrellas from traveling into the house with a built-in bench seat/chest/coat rack combo for mudroom duties. Specialized cabinets with integral storage are also available for sports gear, from soccer and tennis balls to skis and poles.

Above **Combining under-stairs drawers, over-appliance shelves, and a traditional desk gives a small-space basement ample storage room.**

Opposite **A family studio for laundry and hobbies makes use of standard overhead cabinets, a counter with lower cabinets and drawers, a work desk, and a mobile cabinet cart to provide flexibility utility for multitasking.**

Behind Closet Doors

The days of closets with single wooden rods and shelves have long passed. In their place are well-organized systems that provide space for folded and hung clothes, linens, games, books, even toys. Because closet systems take advantage of every linear foot of space, they are much more efficient than the same span with shelving and rods. They keep clutter to a minimum, either making possible smaller size closets or allowing closets to be reduced in size to give more space to the room.

WALK-IN CLOTHES CLOSETS These closet rooms are extremely popular for master bedrooms, even in some guest bedrooms. When poorly designed, however, they can be major space wasters in a smaller home. Like with the other closets of the house, it's important to design walk-ins with maximum linear footage for greatest efficiencies. Use closet systems to increase capacity and include specialized units such as chests, shoe racks, dressing mirrors, makeup vanities, or a small desk.

Closet systems are available in either open-shelving or closed wardrobe-cabinet styles. Of the two, closed cabinets look better and provide superior protection from insects and dust, but they are much more costly than the open alternative. Open systems have the added benefit of being more flexible than closed cabinets. Either system offers similar features, including built-in drawers, bins, trays, and counters for folding or setting out garments. Consider a closed-wardrobe system only if it's necessary to combine uses in the walk-in closet, such as incorporating a home office or a dressing space.

In rooms with high ceilings, you can add a third hanging level and a retractable rod arm that lowers the clothes to eye level for convenient access.

Left Nurseries require temporary storage solutions that change as children grow. Shelf-and-drawer inserts for standard clothes closets are flexible and efficient, and they can be removed at a later date.

Opposite Suspending wall-mounted cabinet units within a closet gives it more storage room than will a standard clothes rod and single overhead shelf. To hang garments, mount stacked rods on the end walls and between the cabinet insert and the wall. Use the interior of the unit, its top, and other shelves for stackable crates and bins or folded apparel. Mount basket bins beneath the unit as a place to hold occasional-use items.

OTHER CLOSETS Closets used for bed and bath linens and those used for general storage also benefit from applying organization techniques, and in each case the space savings are significant. The advantage comes from using the entire vertical space and any available sidewalls, rather than just part of them.

Start by thinking in terms of zones, a series of closets with single purposes. Grouping similar items in a zone makes storage more efficient, and it makes retrieval and use easier. If all your bedding is stored in one closet near the bedrooms, for instance, extra trips to other areas of the house will be unnecessary. Build a satellite linen closet into a Jack-and-Jill bathroom that serves two bedrooms, rather than using space in either bedroom's closet or in an adjacent hall.

Infant nurseries and young children's rooms need more storage space than those for older children, but such needs are frequently short-lived. Plan convertible space that adjusts to new needs as children grow, or install wall shelves and a temporary cabinet within an open closet shell, converting the space inside back to other configurations when the cabinet's usefulness ends.

A small front-entry closet is a helpful place to receive guests' coats. Plan another for the family's main entry door, or mudroom. Include a general storage closet near the family room.

JUST STUFF Continuing the zone concept, make specialized storage space available for other household needs: food pantries, closets for games, cabinets for CDs, and DVDs, and utility closets that hold cleaning equipment and materials. Provide for equipment such as seasonal clothing, holiday decorations, winter sports gear, and pool toys in low-use areas such as attics or basements.

Where closets and cabinets won't fit, try hidden storage as another space-saving option. Use otherwise wasted areas such as drawers beneath platform beds, chests in window seats, niches in wall cavities, or the space under decks.

The areas by garage and back doors deserve special attention because they frequently collect clutter. Organize these spaces with racks, cubbies, cabinets, and shelves.

Left Back doors and the entries from garages naturally become cluttered over time. Organize them with hangers for coats, places for shoes, and cubbies for sports gear. A storage bench is a convenient spot to change shoes or boots.
Right Low-profile drawers on slides make multipurpose storage of mixed-height objects possible. The drawers hide out of sight behind a cabinet door.
Opposite Entry storage needs are solved with a valet station to receive mail, pay bills, study, or enjoy a hobby.

Every family, it seems has a problem keeping everyone's wallets, car keys, and mail from cluttering the kitchen counter. Plant a family valet near the garage entry or hall. These multipurpose built-ins provide personalized storage for each family member and desk space for mail sorting or bill payment. Similar built-ins for homework, e-mail, and message centers can be tucked away under stairs, in alcoves, or in a quiet corner of the house.

In other rooms, specialized cabinetry—built-ins, butler's pantries, wine cellars, wet bars, buffets, library shelves, and media cabinets—provide storage and service areas. They are frequently more economical than traditional freestanding furniture, and they save space. If you prefer freestanding cabinets, construct them of simple drywall columns or assemble prebuilt basic cabinets and shelving units, adding applied millwork to dress them up. Either approach yields an elegant and refined appearance.

Above The wall and base cabinets at left and the recessed built-in hutch in the right corner of this room use doors and pulls that match the freestanding chest of drawers. The hutch allows the side entry door to swing fully open and saves room inside.

Opposite A full-featured desk with computer, screen, keyboard, printer, and other miscellaneous storage resides within a cabinet. With its doors closed, the cabinet resembles a wardrobe or armoire.

Left Wisteria climbs an arbor in front of a cabana with an area to grill and serve light meals at poolside. Such structures add versatility during seasons spent living outdoors.

Opposite Folding doors open to reveal the outdoor kitchen. Its serving bar contains cabinets for plates, cutlery, pots, pans, and serving utensils, while a refrigerator is used for storing perishable food and cold beverages.

Outdoor and Garage Storage

As you incorporate the outdoors into the living area of your home, you'll need to plan for storage of the various tools and materials used for gardening and yard maintenance in the outdoor and garage areas of your home.

YARD STRUCTURES Incorporate yard, patio, and pool storage and the places where it's needed in order to deal with such items as table and chair sets, lounges, barbecues, umbrellas, and propane heaters during the off seasons. The storage area can be in a corner of a lanai, or a freestanding yard structure such as a cabana, or potting shed. Invest in space to stow lawn furniture, cushions, and floats from the elements; they'll last longer and provide better value.

A mini-greenhouse serves double duty: throughout the gardening season, it nurtures tender seedlings and tropical plants; in autumn and winter, it is a secure storage spot for everything needed to garden the following year. Add an outdoor tool shed to hold yard tools, and keep sharp implements, fertilizers, and other garden chemicals away children and pets in locked cabinets.

TOOL RACKS Simple-to-install fixtures extend the function of permanent yard structures by converting their eave-protected walls into hanging storage areas. Locking brackets hang rakes, hoes, spades, and other tools out of the weather. Clip-on brackets support shelves and hose reels. If the structure's overhang is wide enough, vertical bicycle racks, wheelbarrows, and garden carts all can be hung on walls.

Left The benefits of a slot-wall garage storage system are its great storage capacity, flexibility, and clean appearance.
Opposite This garage has room for gardening and woodworking tools plus appliances, yet still has more than enough room to accommodate its automobiles. Using a slot-wall system in your garage means that bulky sports gear will have a perfect home outside of your house interior.

ORDERLY GARAGES Garages carry a heavy load of large storage items, from mowers to sporting goods. This is compounded when insufficient interior storage space in the house causes seldom-used items to migrate into the garage. The single purpose of having a garage—to store and maintain cars—is lost.

Fortunately, flexible cabinetry and storage options exist that remedy many of the downsides that trouble fixed custom cabinetry. Slot-wall storage systems and movable cabinetry are two choices.

Several manufacturers make garage systems based on slot-and-key technology similar to the display systems found in many stores, including the popular system shown here. The first element of a slot-wall system is a series of interlocking horizontal panels that mount firmly to the garage walls. Each panel has slats with a center slot channel running its length that enables it to support substantial weight. Special fixtures fit into the slot like a key into a lock and tighten to grip both sides of the slot.

With the panels in place, simply lift a cabinet to the proper height, slide its keys into the panel slots, and lock it in place. To move it to a new spot, repeat the process—the storage becomes flexible and convenient. With cabinets suspended from the wall instead of resting on the floor, you'll have room for workbenches, power tools, and many other common garage-storage items, including your family automobile. Suspended cabinets also make cleaning the garage floor a snap because the floor beneath them remains open so brooms and mops can pass by freely.

Besides their suspended cabinets, these slot-wall garage systems include roll-about cabinets, toolboxes, and drawer units, plus appliances suited for garage use. Slot-mounted hangers and shelves support everything from leaf blowers and electrical cords to stepladders. The overall effect of a slot-wall system is as visually pleasing as it is efficient for providing storage in a garage, basement, or utility building.

By specifying a slot-wall system in your house's plan prior to construction, you ensure that your garage walls will be finished in an attractive manner, yet the easily removed panels still allow quick access for electrical or plumbing repairs.

Left A neatly-organized garage has room for an automobile as well as your possessions. Use of standard cabinets and lockers removes clutter. Base cabinets fitted with countertops make improvised workbenches , and roller carts are a good choice for storing tools and equipment.

Opposite (clockwise from top left) Overhead storage racks and wall brackets take lightweight, bulky items off of the garage floor. The overhead racks are mounted high enough for people and cars to pass beneath. Stepladders take little space when they are hung flush against the wall. Use storage baskets for loose items. Slot-wall systems also have slot bars to made especially to fit their equipment hangers, suitable for everything from lawnmowers to bicycles.

Other than the slot-wall systems, the most common choice for garage storage is usually a combination of permanent cabinetry and workbenches. If you carefully plan the options, fixed custom cabinetry and benches can provide the most storage possible for any given amount of space. Expansion and modification of fixed cabinets is difficult, however, and they are often too inflexible to solve the changing needs of a family as it grows or its interests change. In many households, the need for a golf-bag locker or a wardrobe for ski attire wanes over the span of a few years, yet custom units usually stay in place long after the family has moved on to new pursuits.

Another answer to garage clutter is overhead storage. Suspend hanging racks from rafters well above normal head height to create storage locations for lightweight, bulky objects such as holiday lights, camping equipment, and empty coolers. Mount narrow over-head racks in the space above overhead garage doors, an ideal spot for storing flat boxes.

To hang heavier items overhead, discuss using engineered beams and trusses with your designers: they'll make sure the structure's framing and walls are strong enough to support brackets for lumber, machine parts, and similar items.

A final option is to take advantage of the wide array of specialty wall hangers to suspend bicycles, wagons, garden carts, mowers, and the like. Each particular hanger provides a custom solution to a specific storage need, so choose hardware systems based on the individual items you plan to store.

Methods of equipping a smaller home with ample storage space and using innovative solutions are seen in the residence that follows on pages 122 to 123.

Above top A cabinet concealed behind a frosted-glass frame stores audio and video media on the wall next to a television used for watching movies.

Above left A hassock-chest holds children's toys when they are not being used.

Above right A built-in platform for a washer-dryer pair raises them to a level convenient for working and makes room for storing laundry baskets beneath.

Right top and bottom With a nod to Japanese culture, a shoe nook next to the main entry and a coat rack helps keep the house clean by stopping dust and mud at the front door.

Opposite left and right Windows arranged in series of repeating geometric groups bring unity to the home's living and dining rooms. Note the wall niches in the dining room repeat the windows' form.

Iverson Residence

Eugene, Oregon. Stephen H. Wright, Oak Tree Builders

The owner-designed custom home seen here and on pages 56 and 124 is 2,217 square feet (206 meters^2), has three bedrooms and two and one-half baths in a generally open plan, and also includes other specialized rooms. The house has many innovative, space-saving storage features, and it works efficiently for the owners and their family. Careful attention provides quality detailing in its arches, niches, lighting, and cabinetry.

Repeating motifs in the house are its use of rectangular, deeply recessed windows with matching cutouts and insets. Triangular repeating forms result from vaulted ceilings and windows arranged in symmetrical patterns. The spacious windows open the home to the surrounding forest on a lot of 6,900 square feet (641 meters^2).

A sense of balance fuses the house's mix of modern and traditional materials, neutral colors, and architectural elements, yet it retains a clean and simple overall feeling.

Throughout the house, the rooms are flexible. Much of the cabinetry and storage is achieved through built-ins that help keep furniture to a minimum. The rooms include reading nooks, places for hobbies, spots to gather as a family to watch motion pictures—a favorite pastime—and listen to music, a laundry, and a home office. A walkway bridge spans and overlooks the great room, uniting the upstairs and downstairs areas.

The result is a carefully considered home that perfectly fits the needs and activities of the active family that resides within its walls and reflects the region in which it was built. The house is a snug and comfortable refuge in Oregon's four-season climate.

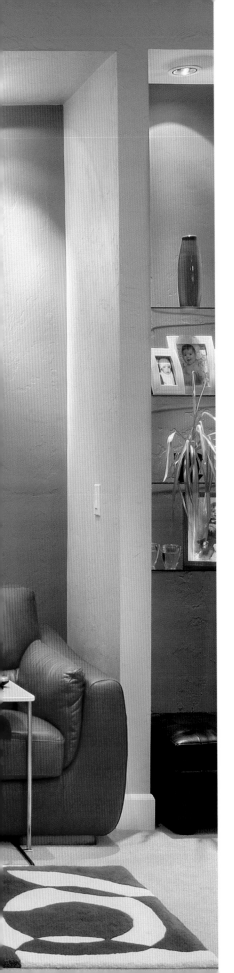

Technology—Home to Stay

The greatest influence on modern residential design results directly or indirectly from the enduring march of technology. In turn, two big trends in technology are ever-smaller sizes and lower prices; new components are vastly more powerful yet even more miniaturized versions of those of previous generations. They often combine several once-separate functions and features into single pieces of equipment, yet are more economical than ever before, and they impact nearly every room of the house. As a result, homes are more affordable, trouble-free, and convenient for their occupants. Technology affects building techniques and nearly every element of a modern home. It improves energy conservation and efficiency, frees more time for leisure-time activities, and, most important, saves space as never before.

A side benefit of employing new technology in a home is the potential for saving space throughout the dwelling. Whether it's saving a few inches (centimeters) along the entire length of a wall by tucking blinds between window panes rather than hanging draperies from a rod or opening up new floor space by stacking laundry and kitchen appliances, the net result is a smaller home with the same or even greater functionality than could exist in its traditional counterpart.

Opposite **The great room of the Iverson residence includes this media wall (see also pages 122 and 123). Above the fireplace is a flat-panel television set in a niche, with media cabinets to each side of the main screen. The wall also contains the front elements of a surround-sound sound speaker array with tweeters and a sub-woofer. Used for watching movies and sports events, the room has every desirable feature of a home theater without overwhelming a multifunctional room used for many other purposes.**

Above left Provide security for your home and get a preview of callers with a closed-circuit TV system. A weatherproof camera mounts over the door and broadcasts its signal to the house's wireless entertainment network controller.

Above right Within the house, any TV screen displays the closed-circuit camera's picture.

Opposite Rather than running a tap until hot water reaches it from the house's water heater or using a stove or microwave oven to heat water for tea, instant beverages and soups, save energy by mounting an instant hot-water dispenser under each sink.

The Integrated Home

The winds of technological change perhaps blow fastest in that arena called the integrated home—with electronic connectivity systems uniting information, entertainment, security, and control systems in a seamless, often wireless, package that extends beyond the walls to the yard and the outside world. An integrated home seems to sense its occupants' needs in a manner that seems partly science fiction and partly wish-come-true. Temperature sensors note that a room is becoming too warm and automatically lower blinds to block warming rays of the sun or opens vents and windows to reduce household cooling expense. Appliances receive instructions from the Internet or a cell phone to start cooking meals during the commute from

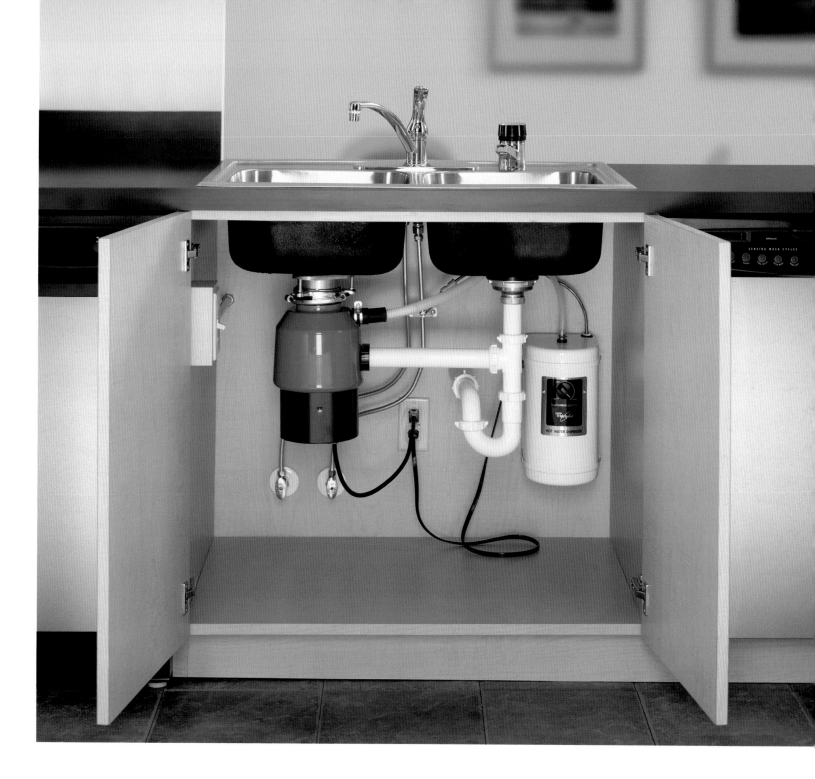

work. As natural light fades, artificial lights turn on automatically, follow occupants from room to room, and turn off behind them as they depart. Water is instantly heated to a preset ideal bathing temperature as soon as the tap turns on. Distributed audiovisual systems allow groups in various parts of the home to share entertainment even as another individual enjoys a custom-tailored program of music or television. Security sensors note intruders before they reach the house, monitoring and recording their actions. The integrated home is here now, ready for the real world and real lives.

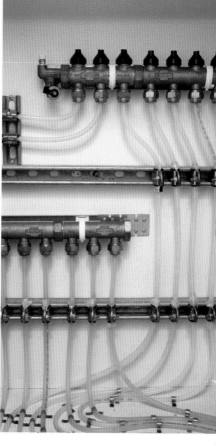

Sight Unseen

If technology affects the house as a whole, it also modifies and alters every room, from kitchen and great room to bathroom, bedroom, and laundry. Radiant-heat floors and walls add luxury while they subtract the space in walls and ceilings, and they are more efficient. Liquid-crystal light panels eliminate overhead fixtures and occasional lamps, provide glare-free illumination, and also save energy. On-demand water heaters concealed in kitchen and bath cabinets eliminate the need for bulky central heaters and costly dual runs of copper pipe to service hot and cold taps; they consume energy only for the short time in which they are supplying unlimited streams of hot water, saving both water and energy.

Examine room by room how these and other technological innovations make the home smaller, smarter, and more efficient yet emphatically more livable.

Above left Radiant floor heating systems warm rooms by circulating water from a central water heater through thin tubes set between subfloors and the finish flooring. **Above right** A hot-water manifold located in a central utility closet divides the heated water's flow to each circuit of floor tubing. **Opposite** A radiant floor requires specialized equipment to heat and store the water it uses. The small box at left is a highly efficient gas-fired water heater. It stores heated water in the reservoir tank seen at right. Circulating pumps pressurize the system, which supplies hot water both to the floor and for other household uses.

Above (clockwise from top left)

Automation technology makes it possible to control an entire house's lighting, heating, entertainment, and information systems with a remote control, a computer, or a series of wall-mounted panels.

A central system controls ceiling fans, household lighting fixtures, air and heating vents, as well as media systems.

Whole-House Technology

Think of household systems while planning the use of technology in your smaller and smarter home. Automate its lighting controls, heating and cooling systems, communications and entertainment electronics, security, and home maintenance.

LIGHTING Apply smart controls to light fixtures, using off-the-shelf sensor switches that detect motion and judge ambient light, have preset dimmers that adapt to general- and task-lighting situations, or respond to controls from a central computer. Save space with flush-to-ceiling or wall-mounted liquid-crystal panels that provide bright illumination and skimp on energy.

PLUMBING Eliminate space-consuming, energy-wasting water heaters with compact, instant-hot units near each sink, tub, shower, or appliance.

HEATING AND AIR-CONDITIONING Radiant-heat tubing in floors and walls eliminates the need for radiators, floor or wall vents, and bulky air ducts; choose a system that's compatible with roof-mounted solar panels, existing boilers, and water heaters. Mount electronic thermostats in each room and in attic spaces to control temperature zone by zone; program them to automatically raise and lower window shades and awnings, start and stop attic exhaust fans, and open and close windows and vents, as well as start and stop the heating and air-conditioning system's furnace and heat pump.

ELECTRONIC CONTROLS Wireless controllers linked to a master computer coordinate appliances, systems, and fixtures. Include a unified communications, entertainment, computing, and security network for telephones, intercoms, audio and television programming, home office functions, and safety monitoring. Such systems deliver entertainment, phone calls, and information to every room of the home.

Above Wireless networks broadcast computer data, audio, and video within a home and to its surrounding yard from a central server. In each room, a control panel selects from the data streams and libraries of stored on-demand programming.
Left These wide-area networks permit each user to have a room-by-room choice for each type of entertainment they access, so viewers have different viewing and listening options or can simultaneously access the Internet.

Above Whole-house vacuums have outlets at several points in the house and powerful central canisters to collect debris. They exhaust outdoors.

Right Natural light is a welcome addition to bathrooms and walk-in closets. Light pipes that collect sunlight and reflect it down into the room through the ceiling give full-spectrum illumination for applying makeup.

Opposite A between-the-pane blind system that raises from the bottom of the window to its top provides privacy without requiring the space from the room used by traditional window coverings.

WINDOWS Dual- and triple-paned windows are energy-efficient; choose models that have integral blinds between their panes to save the space used by traditional draperies and window coverings. Shutters and storm windows reap additional energy savings. In hot climates, apply reflective film coatings to windows to reflect sunlight and filter out harmful UV rays. For privacy in bathrooms and bedrooms, consider liquid-crystal-coated window systems that turn from clear to translucent to opaque at the flip of a switch.

MAINTENANCE Extend the life of floor coverings with a powerful and efficient whole-house vacuum system. Its canister mounts in a basement or attached garage; pipes in the walls lead to convenient outlets where you plug in the hose and tools.

Whole-house technology makes a smaller home smarter—more functional, more convenient, and more economical.

Above top **Decorative range hoods and pot-filling faucets respectively bring elegance and practical function to a cooktop.**
Above bottom **Most stove and hood systems are matched in appearance to bring uniformity to the kitchen's major appliances.**
Right **Island ranges and cooktops use downdraft ventilation systems that either are an integral part of the stove or that pop up from the counter surface when in use, as is demonstrated here.**

What's Cooking in Kitchens?

Promises that date back to black-and-white science-fiction TV shows are about to be fulfilled. A new generation of artificial-intelligence household appliances has made its debut.

High-tech appliances include refrigerators that warn when the produce and fruit they contain become overripe and microwaves and convection ovens that read scanner codes on groceries and tailor their cooking programs to match. Induction cooktops are cool to the touch but instantly heat pans set on their surface.

The many forms and reduced sizes of kitchen appliances are even more exciting for the smaller home. Looking for the oven, refrigerator-freezer, or dishwasher? Pull out the drawers of the food preparation island and behold—they've moved under counter to free up space for more cabinets and storage. Tired of bulky kitchen hoods and want more shelves? Choose a down-drafting cooktop with a powerful venting fan panel that pops up from the rear wall when it's needed.

Even the division between appliances has blurred. Ovens hold assembled but uncooked food dishes, then turn on and bake at the touch of a finger, on the signal of a timer, or on command from a computer, phone, or the Internet. Other oven models combine standard heat with convection, microwave, or steam. Microwaves are paired with toaster ovens, coffee and espresso machines, even television sets. Hang them under cabinets, set them in niches, or build them into the previously wasted corner spaces of kitchen cabinets. Look for new, innovative pairings and other combination appliances as technology makes them possible.

Divide and conquer: rather than using a large, all-in-one refrigerator-freezer plumbed with ice and water, install a dispenser for cold and hot water plus ice in the wasted space on the cabinet front found between the kitchen sink and the cabinet doors below it, then relocate and downsize the refrigerator. At the same time, replace a bulky bottled-water unit with a reverse-osmosis filtration system plumbed into your kitchen sink. Mount a motor flush into the countertop surface to power all your kitchen tools: food processors, mixers, blenders, can openers, and ice crushers.

Left Drawer dishwashers placed by a preparation sink make for a useful workstation on an island. The two drawers have different capacities and can be run either individually or simultaneously, allowing cooks to keep up with a steady stream of dirty dishes while they cook and have free space for serving dishes when the meal ends.

Right Capacity to entertain and cook are hallmarks of this kitchen. Its island is equipped with a built-in trash compactor, drawer dishwashers and refrigerators, a sleek stainless-steel work surface with a built-in double sink, and seating for guests to socialize as the meal is prepared. At the counter's end is the cooktop, while across the alley are pairs of ovens and the main refrigerator/freezers. Low-voltage halogen lighting fixtures provide task lighting.

Opposite Specialty appliances make sense in a home-gourmet setting. Here, a deep fryer is built into the countertop, as is a deep pot-filling sink. The sink has two faucets. One is used to quickly fill utensils and rinse vegetables; the other provides filtered drinking water from a reverse-osmosis water-purification system.

Kitchen Convenience

Establishing a trio of workstations in the kitchen and discarding the kitchen triangle concept—the idea that minimizing the combined distance between the stove, sink, and refrigerator made for greater efficiency—frees space for technology in each workstation: preparation, cooking, and serving.

PREPARATION AREAS At prep sinks and counters, install hands-free controls or motion sensors on pot-filling faucets. It will eliminate the endless cycle of wiping handles clean and yield a bit more space on the sink ledge. Those who have a tendency to pace in front of the microwave can save or eliminate cooking time altogether with instant-hot taps that deliver boiling water for quick-to-prepare foods and hot beverages.

Mount a drawer refrigerator under the counter to keep produce fresh and quick at hand. A drawer dishwasher nearby washes cutlery and crockery. Install a flush-surface food processor motor on the countertop, or place it on a pull-out/swing-up arm built into the counter front; store processor attachments in the cabinets below or in an appliance garage in front of the splash.

For a retro look, add a pull-down, under-cabinet book holder for cookbooks—or go state-of-the-art with a flip-down computer display and keyboard for access to the Internet for recipes or to show videos that reveal meal-planning hints and cooking tips.

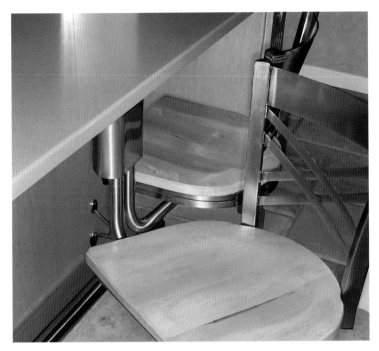

COOKING AREAS In active cooking areas, separate cooktops and ovens and choose multiple-function units. There will be more space for storage, and you will find it easier to work with another cook without conflicts. Modular cooktops and ranges have easily swapped components, ranging from deep fryers to woks, as well as common burners. Save space for more kitchen cabinets by choosing units that incorporate downdraft ventilation systems, or install a back-of-stove pot-filling spout to eliminate trips to the sink.

SERVING AREAS For serving stations, use specialty cabinets that allow you to pull overhead shelves down to eye level and raise lower units to counter height, have sliding shelves or roundabouts for appliances and pans, or hold spices, canisters, and staples on the backs of cabinet doors. Use space-saving options and your cabinets will store up to three times as many kitchen utensils and food staples as those with standard shelves.

Move from kitchen to place setting with an eat-in kitchen equipped with spring-loaded, suspended seats that pull out for dining but collapse and hide beneath the counter after meals. Every smaller kitchen becomes more efficient with technology.

Top Swing-away spring-loaded counter seats borrow industrial design's versatility for the home. In the recessed position, the seats take a fraction of the space of bar stools and float above the floor for quick cleanups.

Opposite New appliance surfaces meld the gap between enamel and stainless steel. They are easy to wipe down and have lasting beauty, yet are neutral in a setting of traditional wood cabinets. This deep gray finish, called Meteorite by its manufacturer, is available for home use in their professional-grade line of appliances.

Left The home theater shown here and on pages 140 and 141 has touches reminiscent of Greek and Italian classic themes made possible by its use of twin columns and gently curved arches. The upstairs theater's walls are sound-proofed, as are the tightly sealed double doors that lead from it to an office and bedroom. It is over the garage.

Opposite (clockwise from top left) An overhead view reveals the basic simplicity of the great room's plan yet exposes its design. The gently curved chimney has a lighted niche and mantle that focuses attention on a Roman bust. Space for an upstairs home office was provided by adding a dormer to the house's roof. The kitchen laptop data dock and bill-paying station is backlit with natural light but retains its privacy through use of a textured-glass window. Swinging corner mounts mounts on the wall allow the TV monitor in the kitchen to swivel for easy viewing throughout the room.

Private Residence

Eugene, Oregon. Oak Tree Builders

The technology-minded owners of this custom home of 2,571 square feet (239 meters^2) wanted a home that reflected their twin loves of sports and staying abreast of current events. The resulting three-bedroom, two and one-half bathroom house has Italian-modern flair and video screens in nearly every room of the home. From a television on the kitchen counter used to watch cooking shows while preparing meals to over-tub screens and offices and bill-paying stations connected to the World Wide Web, both owners' interests are covered in high-definition video and data displays.

For serious sports viewing and to watch motion pictures, the home has a dedicated home theater with a projection television, surround-sound audio, and comfortable theater seats. Special media cabinets on the room's walls hold prerecorded videos, and the room's lighting is computer-controlled with presets to provide the right ambient light for viewing and conversation.

Above Special swinging, double-sided shelves within cabinet doors hold video movies, yet still give easy access to the electronic components behind. Drawers beneath have room for more video programs.

Right top The projection television is mounted on the ceiling.

Right bottom Three upholstered, reclining theater seats are set at an ideal viewing distance from the projection television's screen.

Opposite When it's in use, the room provides a theaterlike experience of video and sound.

Relax in Leisure

The hub of an American home is a place in which to share time with family, relax, and entertain or be entertained. In smaller homes, the preferred spot for family gatherings is the great room—usually a multifunctional space with eat-in kitchen or dining room. It's also a top spot to find fresh technology.

From home theater to interactive media centers, passive entertainment takes center stage in a room where leisure is the foremost consideration. Rather than create a separate room to house a television, integrate its functions with a built-in flat-panel screen, wireless network, surround-sound system, and audio/video jukeboxes with a capacity to entertain that exceeds nearly anyone's expectations. Still, you may feel that only a home theater will do.

Pairing recessed flat-panel built-ins or ceiling-projection television sets and new micro-entertainment servers means relegating your space-eating entertainment centers and storage cabinets for video DVDs and music CDs to the past, giving the great room a spare, clean look with more space, greater flexibility in furniture arrangement, and customized usage. Consider replacing that old furniture with a built-in or see-through fireplace for old-fashioned, cozy relaxation and downtime; new models draft to vents—some are even ventless—and can be placed in room dividers or built into cabinets or walls.

Digital video recorders, or DVRs, are a boon for recording and viewing broadcast programming whenever you want. The DVRs equivalents in audio programming are downloadable music and podcast libraries; they'll store thousands of songs or hours of audio programs in a unit small enough to hold in the hand, plus they'll distribute it to every room in the house. Choose a system that is compatible with current—and adaptable to future—video game and HDTV systems.

Prepare the room for high-definition viewing; the standard is in place and soon it will be the most common format. Remember when choosing a video screen that viewing distance relates directly to screen size: the larger the screen, the greater the distance from which you can comfortably view it. A screen too large or too small for the room will be uncomfortable to watch; choose a model appropriate to your room's dimensions, using this rule of thumb: divide the screen's diagonal measure in inches by four to yield the ideal viewing distance in feet (divide centimeters by 33 to give viewing distance in meters).

Because great rooms are used for tasks other than viewing, plan an adaptable, flexible lighting plan suited to a variety of uses. A leisure room is a good place to use switch-activated, mechanized window shades or shutters, especially if it has a high ceiling and tall, out-of-reach windows. The shades will brighten or dim the room during the day, perhaps even adding a measure of insulation to save energy costs.

For artificial light, use both direct and indirect general illumination, include task-lighting fixtures for specific areas, and back-light video screens to eliminate eyestrain during viewing. Install both wall and floor outlets near furniture with occasional and floor lamps. Use electronic lighting controllers to raise or dim each fixture or outlet to fit the needs of varied activities: choose a system with multiple presets and program into them a gallery of lighting plans ideal for the room's every purpose.

A great room is also the right place to install a radiant heat floor. It will add a luxurious and cozy touch to a place where family members will spend many hours. Youngsters love to lounge on

Right Motorized window coverings raise and lower at the touch of a button, or they can be controlled by a computer linked to a light and temperature sensors. These systems make it practical to use window coverings on very tall or highly placed windows that are inaccessible otherwise.

warm, carpeted floors, further adding useful space by reducing furniture to meet seating needs.

Finally, for the ultimate place to lounge, include a built-in wall bar with sink, mini-fridge, beverage dispenser, and microwave for heating snacks. Put an instant-hot/chilled water tap at the sink, and you'll see less kitchen traffic during meal-preparation times.

Customize leisure space. If fitness is a priority, build in storage for exercise machines. Like table games? Locate them on a peripheral edge or in a nook. If big groups will gather and watch games, include theater seating. Much time will be spent in your family or club room, so fit it to needs and activities.

Above Other features extend the traditional functions of a library. Adding a television and electronic components in its built-in shelves and cabinets makes it into an entertainment center. Glass shelving, a mini-refrigerator, and a sink add bar amenities. The result is a clublike atmosphere.

Above Modern laundry rooms have ironing stations and clothes freshening appliances besides their standard washer and dryer.

Practically Clean

Another technology-rich area worth considering is the laundry and utility room. Adding functional appliances and features to these rooms moves activities from the house's main living areas to a central, out-of-traffic location.

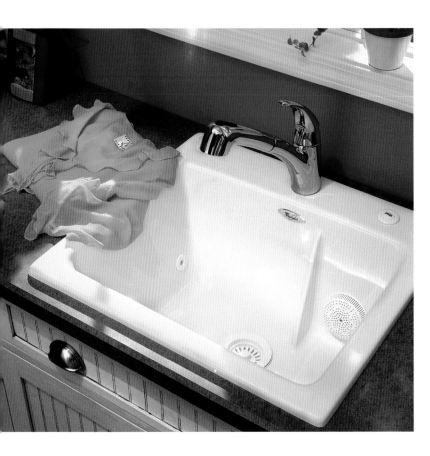

Helping to configure a utility room to respond to specific needs for cleaning, laundering, hobbies, and homework are an array of high-tech appliances and fixtures. Save space by dispensing with a paired washer and dryer. Install a single machine that both washes and dries—it takes a load of clothes from dirty-and-dry to dry-and-clean—or choose stackable pairs to save floor space. Still another option is downsized washer-dryer pairs—many so-called apartment models exist.

Most of these appliances are environment-friendly and conserve water and energy. Regardless of which you select, more labor-saving equipment will fill the saved space: sorting tables, touch-up stations, wall- or door-mounted folding ironing boards, and clothes steamers. Give delicates a gentle whirlpool bath in a jet-equipped laundry sink and dry them on a retractable clothesline or a fold-down rack to free the master bathroom forever from the clutter of rinsed lingerie and hosiery. Freshening units even renew dry-clean-only garments and woolens, adding cycles of wear without laundering.

Left Jetted laundry sinks make washing delicates as breeze. Air pumped through the water in the sink gently agitates delicates without stretching or damage. **Above** Where space is needed, use stacking appliances to give full laundry capacity to a small utility room. Here, it was possible to add a stall shower once the washer-dryer pair was stacked.

Above top An eye-catching way to provide a soft night light in a bathroom is by using a cast-glass vanity sink lit from below.

Above bottom High-tech toilets have a variety of functions, from warm water jets to air blowers.

Right The under-cabinet lighting in this bathroom senses movement and turns on as a night light. The faucets are equipped with similar sensors that turn on water at a preset temperature, then turn it off when use is finished.

Opposite left If you prefer relaxing by soaking in the swirling waters of a whirlpool tub, choose a tub model that is sufficiently deep and which has its own water heater, since the hot water quickly cools in those that lack a heater.

Opposite right Bathing takes on an entirely new meaning in a shower fitted with a hand wand and body-surrounding, multiple showerheads.

Technology Takes to the Bath

The final stop on this technology tour is in your bathroom. The era of low-consumption toilets that didn't flush on the second or third try are long past. Choose an efficient one that is compact rather than extended in length and make more room; tall models give stiffened knees a break, and some deluxe models even rinse and blow dry, ever so gently.

Apply the same principles to the tub and shower. Weigh carefully the need for a Roman bath-sized whirlpool: will an extra-deep round tub for soaking fill the bill at a fraction of the footprint, or would a shower alone suffice? The space saved might even allow room for a steam-shower combination.

Keep the bathroom light and airy yet private with windows equipped with liquid-crystal-coated glass that switch from clear to translucent in an instant.

Bathrooms are also the right place to install motion-sensing faucets, recirculating hot-water or instant-hot-water systems, and automatic temperature controllers. Warm vanity mirrors to evaporate mist, heat bath sheets, and install a pull-down, built-in hair dryer for the ultimate in spa luxury at home.

Choosing features from the broad spectrum of technology for your smaller home takes you another step toward making it smarter: more practical, efficient, luxurious, and customized to the way you really live. Over the lifetime of the house, it will work together with all the other elements specified by your design team.

The final step to having the dream home you want is to make those decisions that affect and impact both the house and you for years to come, building long-term value into your smaller home.

Hidden Value:
Quality for the Long Term

Like many others, our home in southwest Florida has experienced hurricanes. As Charlie passed, I felt concern for the homes I designed on the beachfront near the eye's path. It was with relief and satisfaction that I discovered how well they had survived. Our investments in quality materials and construction paid off, as other homes suffered major damage.

Building quality into a smaller and smarter home requires more than finding an innovative design that carefully matches the home's features to your list of needs and wants. Achieving lasting quality also means investing in construction materials and components that will add value over the house's lifetime.

Major structural systems and materials such as the foundation, exterior finish, roofing, insulation, and windows are difficult to replace. Instruct your design team to choose only those components that perform well and are long-lasting. A kitchen counter can be easily replaced, but laying a new foundation requires hard and costly work. Low-quality windows may seem a bargain, but when higher heating costs occur due to poor insulation, gas seals fail requiring window replacement, or expensive furnishings fade when the windows fail to block the sun's ultraviolet rays, the economic illusion falls away and the true cost is revealed.

Opposite A wealth of detail is evident in the smaller home seen here and on pages 152 to 155. The sandblasted ceiling beams in the dining room provide contrast to the refined arch motif that was used to divide this open plan. Hand-painted murals were used along with sponging to add interest to the round-cornered, thin-set plaster walls, emphasized by directional lighting on dimmer presets. In the case of this home's major living zone, these elements unify the room's areas yet keep their three use areas separate and distinct.

Trade-offs

Faced with a tight budget, it's easy to make the common mistake of sacrificing important structural elements of the house in favor of purely cosmetic ones. In the long run, though, items such as a media-center television have short lives compared to quality doors, floors, or bathroom fixtures.

When evaluating which elements to stress, remember that some rooms in the house will quickly become dated and need refreshing. The most frequently remodeled rooms in most houses are kitchens, bathrooms, and bedrooms. Knowing that sinks, counters, cabinet faces, and appliances are likely to be replaced in seven to ten years, you might see the sense of installing life-time components elsewhere in the house.

Seek out economical alternatives to stretch your budget and make possible using quality materials and systems where they are needed. Cement-fiber siding, for example, is an inexpensive

Your choices of flooring materials have two objectives: uniting and separating areas while providing long-term value and quality.

Left top Heavy traffic areas of the home have limestone pavers set diagonally. Use of diagonally set stone is repeated in bathrooms.

Left bottom Strip hardwood floors are a wear-resistant and durable answer for hallways. Again, the flooring is laid in a diagonal pattern. To soften the effect of the wood, the adjacent dining room area has a large area rug to add a splash of deep color.

Right Carpeting on stairs and bedroom areas was placed on a thick carpet pad so as to reveal the underlying hardwood flooring.

Opposite Transitions from stone to wood and changes of level divide the open main gallery into its entry and living spaces. Note that the bullnosed stone steps are curved in an arch that repeats the patterns seen overhead in the arches on the ceiling shown on the previous pages.

alternative to wood. It has provided such savings in residential construction that it has become a popular substitute. Or, use faux-paint techniques to add texture and interest to a wall or ceiling, but be sure to achieve a professional result that matches the quality of the rest of your home's finishing details.

Also choose durable materials and make plans to maintain them. Quality wood flooring has a lifetime of 25 or more years; ceramic and stone tile, 30 or more years. Compare that to the 10 or 15 years you can expect from vinyl, and 5 to 10 years for carpeting and pad. A wood or tile floor might cost fractionally more to install than a quality wool carpet, but over its lifetime either wood or tile is two to five times more economical than the carpet—and the gap between them widens still further for comparisons made with lower-grade carpeting.

Carmel-by-the-Sea Getaway

Carmel, California. McMills Construction

The owner-designed seaside home seen here and on pages 156 to 159 was built on a narrow, sloping lot typical of this artist's enclave on the California coast. The house is 2,450 square feet (228 meters^2) with minimal setbacks to the sides and rear, and it has two bedrooms and four bathrooms, plus a home office and a single-car attached garage.

The residence is built in three tiers descending from the front entry, giving it three floors but a single-story curbside appearance. Built of traditional wood-frame construction, natural stone facings and quality materials were used throughout the home.

The owners commissioned original wall murals for the main public areas and bedrooms.

Opposite (clockwise from top left)
The built-in pantry/sideboard was customized from stock cabinetry by adding top moldings and doors with leaded stained glass. The kitchen's low ceiling uses the same open beams seen in the dining room (see page 150), and the counter and low soffit with its series of downlights are a visual break from the dining room. The home's rustic stone-veneer finish matches the prevailing architecture used for other Carmel residences. A skylight in the stairwell spills natural light down on both levels of the home.

Left A home office has wainscot paneling and wooden shutters. Use of moldings and a midwall chair rail along with stepped crown moldings give the room its strongly masculine influences.
Right A built-in storage cabinet, shelves, and file drawers satisfy storage needs in the office while making it unnecessary to use furniture for that purpose.

Long-Term Investments

These building materials have economic and strategic values compared to their traditional counterparts:

- Cement-fiber siding: Environment-friendly; lasts longer and has lower maintenance than wood.
- Concrete tile roofs: An attractive, green alternative for wood and asphalt shingle with a lifetime of 40 to 50 years.
- Composite or cast columns: Last longer, look better, and require less maintenance than wood or resin-coated foam.
- Solar panels: Effective and energy efficient—whether used to heat water or generate electricity—and may qualify for rebates or tax exemptions.
- Water-purification systems: Prevent fouling and corrosion of pipes, plumbing systems, and water heaters.
- Insulation: A must-have in every house, with unparalleled energy savings and cost efficiencies.

Left Composite cast columns are a value compared to stone and are more durable than wood. **Above right** Slate tile roofs have a distinctive appearance convincingly captured by this cast tile facsimile. **Opposite** Cement-fiber siding is a natural wood look-alike that makes sense for this house in a warm, moist semitropical setting and extends the structure's expected life. Composed of cement, sand, and cellulose wood fiber cured by steam, it costs less than either wood siding or stucco and will keep its good looks over a planned service life of 50 years. The house also features long-lasting concrete tiles instead of either composition shingles or shakes.

Above Standard in many areas, concrete block foundations and 2×6 exterior framing yield wider wall cavities than is possible with traditional 2×4s that allow you to install extra insulation, making the house more energy efficient.

The Exterior Shell

The exterior walls and roof of a house are its first defense against air infiltration—a prime cause of heat and cold transfer—and the first place to invest in quality.

WALL AND ROOF SYSTEMS In both very hot or cold climates—and elsewhere as recommended—use block, ICF, or 2×6 instead of 2×4 framing; fill the extra space it provides with insulation and keep energy losses to a minimum. Apply tongue-and-groove panel sheathing with screws and glue, and seal every seam and opening. Wrap the entire house in breathable nonwoven fabric to block air infiltration and prevent water from entering yet permit moisture vapor to pass.

units. They pay back their greater initial cost with savings on utility bills over their entire lifetime.

Distributed air-conditioning and heating is also possible using small, self-contained heat pumps to service individual areas of the home. Such systems make heating or cooling the entire structure to comfortable temperature unnecessary in situations where only a few rooms are used extensively for long periods of time.

PLUMBING Reverse-osmosis water-purification systems eliminate particulates and suspended soluble carbonates as well as bacterial and many organic and chemical contaminants. They prevent corrosive damage to water heaters and pipes, stop buildup of sludge in water heaters and pipes, and remove nearly all foul tastes and odors from most water supplies. The reverse osmosis–conditioned water is soft, requiring less detergent and lower temperatures to wash dishes or clothes than hard water.

Instantaneous water heaters mounted in a distributed system at each location of use provide unlimited hot water at preset temperatures for as long as it is needed, reducing energy costs. They also eliminate the need for hot-water-supply pipes or recirculating pipes, since all supply water is cold until it reaches the unit.

Both natural gas and electrical models are available, and either can supplement a solar hot-water system mounted on the roof for even greater energy savings.

Whole-house humidifiers and dehumidifiers extend the range of comfortable temperatures in the house and minimize the frequent problem of electrostatic shock that occurs during dry conditions. In addition, these units filter away or settle dust, helping to keep furniture and floors clean and prevent shrinking, warping, and cracking of fine wooden furniture.

ELECTRICAL SYSTEMS Installing low-voltage lighting systems reduces energy costs, as do liquid-crystal panel lights with low energy needs. As is true for hot-water plumbing, solar panels may be incorporated into a house lighting plan. In this situation, photovoltaic cells generate direct current stored in a battery system. Using a converter, they also can feed power back into the municipal grid and run the electric meter backward when they generate more power than the house uses.

Computer-controlled lighting systems with presets, dimmers, and auto-on/off sensors are more efficient than manual systems and reduce energy costs.

Left **Photovoltaic arrays use semiconductors to generate electrical current directly from sunlight. Power from the array, made up of thousands of silicon chips, produces usable amounts of electricity whenever the panels are bathed in light, even on cloudy days. In sunny climates, an array of the size shown here generates most of the power needed by a single-family home. While costly to install, they reduce energy costs over their long lifetime. Most solar systems are a backup to utility power, but in rural areas they may be the primary source of electricity for a home.**

Right For homes with enthusiastic gourmet cooks, a restaurant-style range with a pot-filler tap above the stove represents practical luxury. It fills heavy stock pots without making a trip to the sink.

Upgrades

Making the house smaller, adopting an open plan, and combining functionality in rooms will free up some of your budget for outfitting and upgrading your home's appointments, including its interior detailing (see High Definition, page 68).

Where are upgrades appropriate, and where should you use them? Return to your priority list for guidance as a starting point. Concentrate on those activities and features that your family particularly enjoys, and note the rooms that receive the most use. If the family cook is a gourmet, it might make sense to upgrade from a regular stove to a professional restaurant-type cooktop, but the difference would be lost on the residents of a home in which meals are mostly from take-out or the microwave. If the family room is the spot that receives the most use, and if watching television dominates, it's an excellent prospect for upgrading with a home theater system. If luxurious bathing in a spalike environment is already routine, an environmental shower with steam and sauna features may give you even more enjoyment.

There are upgrades that make financial sense and those that should be examined more closely. Earlier, in discussing priorities, the short lifetime of a kitchen or bath was noted (see Trade-offs, page 154). Cabinetry is an expensive component of any kitchen,

Left The butcher-block surface of this island makes it practical for preparing meals and eliminates the need for separate cutting boards. Combining drawers and standard cabinets gives the island versatility for storing kitchen appliances, utensils, dishes, and linens. The oversized cut-stone sink can handle the largest stove-top grill or pot, yet communicates the elegance of this family-friendly kitchen.

as are its sinks and appliances. The same holds true for bathroom fixtures. Will these items in either room become dated and be replaced long before their usable life has expired? If so, it's better to go for good basic value rather than lifetime cabinetry.

In a typical kitchen or bathroom, 15 percent or more of its cost may be from the cabinetry and countertops. Appliances may add another 4 to 5 percent to the budget. Since these costs will be rolled into a mortgage that may last 30 to 40 years—more with refinancing—it's possible that the portion of mortgage payments attributable to them might continue long after the rooms have been remodeled and they are gone.

Another measure of upgrades is obsolescence. A few years ago, projection televisions made their way onto the scene. Today, they have been replaced by flat-panel high-definition televisions that far surpass the performance of the old models, and in a few years new broadcasting standards mean that the projection TVs won't work at all. Similarly, wired connectivity is passing the torch to wireless networking that uses radio frequencies to send data instead of wiring. Further examples occur in a variety of other technological applications. If an upgrade is likely to be replaced soon, consider an economical alternative and design in plans for new technology now.

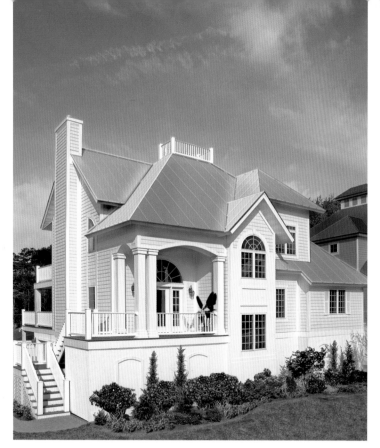

Left This home is 1,886 square feet (174 meters²). Its light-colored, durable, panel-metal roofing is a good choice for homes built in hurricane-prone areas or those seeking to capture a tropical flair. **Right** The exterior of the house shown on the book's cover and on pages 68 to 73 is equiped with a hipped concrete-tile roof. Its drive is paved with interlocking pavers made of concrete block.

Building Equity and Paying Dividends

Throughout this book, the emphasis has been on building or remodeling to create a smaller and smarter house that is highly customized to your needs. You've seen methods to reduce the square footage of your house while retaining all of its essential functionality and features, tailoring it to meet your needs and wants. The result is a highly refined home-design plan executed in tandem with your team of designers, builders, and craftspersons. Like you, your home is personal, tailored, and unique.

Proper investment in good design, quality finishes, and excellent construction for your home brings a phenomenal return on equity and investment that either provides many years of comfortable living for your family or builds value through eventual sale of the property. Whichever of these objectives you seek, friends and potential buyers alike will recognize with desire your well-designed home, noting its personal touches and the features it has that help it fit you like a glove. These very factors are the ones most sought by those seeking smaller homes such as those discussed in these pages.

Craftsmanship is the direct descendent of clearly held standards, which in turn stem from satisfying purpose and fulfilling needs. The emotional energy you expended in the process—to evaluate your lifestyle, prioritize wants, set realizable budgets, assemble your team, create interactive and multifunctional spaces, detail your home, provide ample storage, and adopt quality technology—translates all these things into a workable design that endows your home with elements you find desirable. Quality may be difficult to describe, but it remains easy to recognize, feel, and enjoy.

Your smaller home is also a way of communicating value to other generations. The very act of designing and building is a pursuit you share with all of humankind. You appreciate the result when a craftsperson's hands turn wood, lay stone, hone, paint, and polish. You see the play of light and dark across planes of color, texture, and distance. Every smarter home—whether tiny, midsize, or large—communicates your basic understanding of the important things: home, hearth, and family. Your smaller and smarter house expresses your daily life and true personality, a lasting testament to its value and equity.

Above **This single-story home has three bedrooms and bathrooms and, at 2,885 square feet (268 meters²), is nearly at the top end of a smaller home's size. Its master suite is to the left of the entry and it has two guest suites to the right, while the central main living area features an eat-in kitchen, a formal dining room, a great room with a vaulted ceiling, and a study/den. Twin dormers and a porch with arches, classic columns, pillars of stone, and a custom front door make its face memorable.**

When I first started out, I thought that my work centered on conceiving innovative structures and matching them to their sites. In a short while, I found that my real work involved designing comfortable houses that pleased and fit my clients.

Smaller homes come in many sizes and prices, with each one being as snug as its owners' needs. Each house reflects personality interpreted through individual thoughts, discussion with others, and eventual design, specification, and construction decisions. Each also results from a collaborative effort between the owners and their design and construction team. For that reason, no two residences will be alike. Success in this endeavor is measured by pride of the owners in what they create, the speed at which it becomes a true home, and how quickly it adapts to the way they live their lives.

The process I use to design a smaller home starts and ends with how my clients live within its walls. The end result may be a home for them that is smaller than expected, just as small as planned, or one that is somewhat larger than originally envisioned. Most important, it will be adaptable, highly flexible, and ever tolerant of their changing activities, pastimes, and pursuits. If the outcome of every effort by every contributor is successful, the home will be a mirror that portrays my clients' personalities as well.

A smaller house becomes as vital and alive as its owners.

Left The master bedroom of the home profiled on pages 154 and 155 shows how a single feature of a room can be its focal point. Whether through its graceful lines, central positioning, choice of materials, or the appealing mural that evokes the Spanish mission heritage of California that so influenced its regional setting, this fireplace brings together each element with grace and style.
Opposite The hand-planed wooden mantle of the fireplace invites a touch. Its rich cinnamon color stands in contrast to the prevailing light tones used for the rest of the room.

Resources

American Home Furnishings Alliance
High Point, NC
(336) 884–5000
www.afma4u.org

American Institute of Architects (AIA)
Washington, D.C.
800–AIA–3837 (242–3837)
www.aia.org

American Institute of Building Design (AIBD)
Stratford, CT 06615
(800) 366–2423
www.aibd.org

American Lighting Association
Dallas, TX
(800) BRIGHT IDEAS (274–4484)
www.americanlightingassoc.com

American Society of Interior Designers (ASID)
Washington, D.C.
(202) 546–3840
www.asid.org

American Society of Landscape Architects (ASLA)
Washington, D.C.
(202) 898-2444
www.asla.org

Brick Industry Association
Reston, VA
(703) 620–0010
www.bia.org

Building Stone Institute
Itasca, Illinois
(630) 775–9130
www.buildingstone.org

Cedar Shake & Shingle Bureau
Sumas, WA
(604) 820–7700
www.cedarbureau.org

Composite Panel Association/Composite Wood Council
Gaithersburg, MD
(301) 670–0604
www.pbmdf.com

Copper Development Association
New York, NY
(800) CDA–DATA (232–3282)
www.cda-copper.org

International Code Council
Falls Church, VA
(888) ICC–SAFE (422–7233)
www.iccsafe.org

International Concrete Repair Institute
Des Plaines, IL
(847) 827–0830
www.icri.org

International Wood Products Association
Alexandria, VA
(703) 820–6696
www.iwpawood.org

Metal Roofing Alliance
Belfair, WA
(360) 275–6161
www.metalroofing.com

National Association of Home Builders (NAHB)
(incl. Remodelers Council)
Washington, D.C.
(800) 368–5242
www.nahb.org

National Association of the Remodeling Industry
Des Plaines, IL
(847) 298–9200
www.remodeltoday.com

National Concrete Masonry Association
Herndon, VA
(703) 713–1900
www.ncma.org

National Paint and Coatings Association
Washington, D.C.
(202) 462–6267
www.paint.org

National Sunroom Association
Topeka, KS
(785) 271–0208
www.nationalsunroom.org

Portland Cement Association
Skokie, IL
(847) 966–6200
www.cement.org

Sealant, Waterproofing & Restoration Institute
Kansas City, MO
(816) 472–SWRI (472–7974)
www.swrionline.org

Southern Pine Council
Kenner, LA
(504) 443–4464
www.southernpine.com

Tile Council of North America
Anderson, SC
(864) 646–TILE (646–8453)
www.tileusa.com

Western Wood Products Association
Portland, OR
(503) 224–3930
www.wwpa.org

Window Coverings Association of America
Grover, MO 63040
(888) 298–9222
www.wcaa.org

Window Covering Manufacturers Association
New York, NY
(212) 297–2122
www.wcmanet.org

The Wood Flooring Manufacturers Association
Memphis, TN
(901) 526–5016
www.nofma.org

Wood Promotion Network
Chicago, IL
(866) 275–9663
www.beconstructive.com

Contributors

Balance Associates Architects
Tom Lenchek
Scott Labenz
80 Vine Street, Suite 201
Seattle, WA 98121
206 322–7737
www.balanceassociates.com
Photography by Tom Lenchek, pp. 59, 65 (Top L & R),
    66 (L & Bot R),
Photography by Steve Keating, pp. 5(2nd.), 38–41, 58, 64,
    65 (Bot L & R), 66 (Top R), 67

Brondell, Inc.
A Better Bathroom Experience
2183 Sutter Street
San Francisco, CA 94115
888 542–3355
www.brondell.com
p. 148 (Bot L)

Easy Closets
Your Online Closet Source
20 Stone House Road
Milington, NJ 07946
800 910–0129
www.easyclosets.com
pp. 108–111

Firenze Arts
Shelley Anne Cost
P.O. Box 4073
Monterey, CA 93940
831 375–9477
shelleycost@hotmail.com
Photography by John Rickard, pp. 46, 150–152, 166–167

Group 41 Inc.
Joel M. Karr
3904 17th Street
San Francisco, CA 94114
415 431–0300
www.group41inc.com
joel@group41inc.com
Photography by Victor Wong, pp. 34–35

Hail's Plumbing
William Hail
Mt. Shasta, CA
530 926–2393
Photography by John Rickard, pp. 128–129

Iverson & Company Inc. Realty and Oak Tree Builders
Boyd Iverson, Contractor, Broker
Jordan Iverson, Associate Broker
Stephen H. Wright, Architect
1872 Williamette St.
Eugene, OR 97401
541 284–2524
www.IversonAndCompany.com
Photography by John Rickard, pp. 5(5th.),56, 89, 122–124,
    131, 134 (R), 140–141, 147 (Bot R)

Kraftmaid Cabinetry
P.O. Box 1055
15535 South State Ave.
Middlefield, OH 44062
800 571–1990
fax 440 632 9533
www.kraftmaid.com
pp. 5(4th.), 32, 54, 57, 98–99, 101, 104–107, 114–115,
    162 (Zodiaq® by DuPont. Zodiaq® is a DuPont registered trade-
    mark for its quartz surfaces. Only DuPont makes Zodiaq®.), 163

Leonard Construction
Jason Leonard
Mt. Shasta, CA
530 859–2841
Photography by John Rickard, pp. 50–51

Manhattan Cabinetry
Custom Design Furniture
227 East 59th Street
New York, NY 10022
1 800 manhattan
www.manhattancabinetry.com
info@manhattancabinetry.com
pp. 21, 143

McMills Construction
Corey McMills
105 Fox Hollow Road
Woodside CA 94062
650 941–0946
mcmillsconstruction.com
Photography by John Rickard, pp. 5 (6th), 46–47, 93, 132,
    150–155, 159, 167
Photography by Robert Dolezal, pp. 139, 166

Philip J. Meyer LTD Interior Design
1005 Bush Street
San Francisco, CA 94109
415 673–6984
www.philipjmeyerltd.com
Photography by Kathryn MacDonald, pp. 24–25, 42–43

Pella Windows & Doors™
888–84–PELLA
www.pella.com
Photography by Christine M. Irwine for Pella, p. 133

Sater Design Collection
Dan Sater
25241 Elementary Way, Suite 201
Bonita Springs, Florida 34135–7883
phone: 239 495–5478
saterdesign.com
Photography by Tom Harper, pp. 16, 62, 72–73, 83, 156
Photography by Richard Leo Johnson, cover & pp. 5 (3rd.),
    8–9, 68–71, 157 (L), 168
Photography by Joseph Lapeyra, pp. 63 (Top), 74–75,
    81 (R), 90
Photography by Kim Sargent Photography, pp. 55, 63 (Bot),
    80, 82, 87
Photography by Doug Thompson Photography, pp. 5(1st.), 6–7,
    10–15, 19–20, 28–29, 61, 76–79, 92, 94–97, 164 (L), 165
Photography by CJ Walker, p. 84

Seidel/Holzman Architects
Alexander Seidel, FAIA
Stacy Holzman, PE
545 Sansome Street 9th Floor
San Francisco, CA 94111
415 397–5535
www.seidelholzman.com
mail@seidelholzmn.com
Photography by Russell Abraham, p. 86
Photography by Robert Millman, pp. 26–27
Photography by John Vaughn, p. 91

**Whirlpool Corporation
The Inside Advantage™**
2000 N. M–63
Benton Harbor, MI 49022–2692

Whirlpool® Home Appliances
800–253–1301
www.whirlpool.com
pp. 127, 134 (Bot L), 146, 147(L)

Gladiator GarageWorks®
866 342–4089
www.gladiatorgw.com
pp. 118–119, 121 (Top R & Bot L & R)

KitchenAid® Home Appliances
800–422–1230
www.kitchenaid.com
pp. 134 (Top L), 135–136, 138, 162

Wood-Mode Inc. Fine Custom Cabinetry
One Second Street
Kreamer, PA 17833
800–635–7500
www.wood-mode.com
pp. 102–103, 112–113

Acknowledgments

Special thanks is given to each individual and organization that provided assistance and information during the creation of this book. Our gratitude is also extended to the architects, designers, builders, photographers, and homeowners who shared their projects with our readers. The results demonstrate their exceptional creative arts and crafts.

Thanks is given to the following homeowners:

Steve & Jeanette Hunsaker
Jordan & Shelly Iverson
Robert Karp & Catherine Schmidt
Jason & Janée Leonard
Leland & Sandra Leonard
John & Rika Rickard
Gary & Chris Samuels
Beverly Shannon
Tory Shannon
Bill & Joann Truby
Rocky & Susan Wagner
Keith Wood

Special thanks is given to the following individuals:

Kim Craig, Kraftmaid Cabinetry
Aaron Deetz, Manhatan Cabinetry
Jennifer Emmons, Sater Design
Susan Goldblatt, The Goldblatt Group, Inc.
    for Wood-Mode Inc. Fine Custom Cabinetry
Lori Graybill, Wood-Mode Inc. Fine Custom Cabinetry
John Jaworski, Easy Closets
Jane Johnson, Atlantic Archives
Mark Johnson, Whirlpool Corporation
Alma Mezzell, Sater Design
Jim Van Huysse, Brondell, Inc.

Dolezal & Associates

Book Development Team

President:
  Robert J. Dolezal

Managing Director/Project Manager:
  Barbara K. Dolezal

Editor-in-Chief:
  Victoria Irwin

Art Design:
  Gary Hespenheide
  Hespenheide Design, Newbury Park, CA

Writer:
  Robert J. Dolezal

Photographic Art Director:
  John Rickard
  www.johnrickard.com

Photo Researchers:
  Rich Binsacca
  Barbara K. Dolezal
  Jennifer Emmons
  John Rickard

Photoshop Artist:
  Jerry Bates

This book was produced for Collins Design by

Dolezal & Associates
2176 Crossroads Place
Livermore, CA 94550
(925) 373-3394
www.dolezalpublishing.com

Photo Credits

Dolezal Publishing
John Rickard, Art Director, pp. 5 (5th. & 6th.), 22–23, 30–31, 36–37, 46–51, 56, 81 (L), 85, 88–89, 93, 100, 116–117, 120, 121 (Top L), 122–124, 126, 128–129, 131–132, 134 (R), 137, 140–144, 147 (R), 148 (Top L & R), 149–155, 157 (R), 159, 161, 167
Jerry Bates, Photo Shop Artist, p. 160
Robert J. Dolezal, pp.139, 166

Russell Abraham
309 Fourth Street, Suite 108
Oakland, CA 94607
510 544–5204
www.rabrahamphoto.com
russell@rabrahamphoto.com
p. 86, Courtesy of Seidel/Holzman
Architects (see Contributors)

Brondell, Inc.
p. 148 (Bot L), Courtesy of Brondell, Inc.
(see Contributors)

Easy Closets
pp. 108–111, Courtesy of Easy Closets
(see Contributors)

Heather Fassio Photography
www.hfassio.com
206 799–3232
p. 45

Tom Harper
461 Jung Blvd. E.
Naples, FL 34120
239 560–0994
tom@thomasharper.net
pp. 16, 62, 72–73, 83, 156, Courtesy of Sater
Design (see Contributors)

Christine M. Irvine
p. 133, Courtesy of Pella Windows & Doors
(see Contributors)

Richard Leo Johnson
Atlantic Archives Inc.
415 E. 44th Street
Savannah, GA 31405
912 201–9484
www.atlanticarchives.com
richard@richardleojohnson.com
Cover & pp. 5(3rd.), 8–9, 68–71, 157 (L),
168, Courtesy of Sater Design (see
Contributors)

Steve Keating Photography
5396 East Blaisdell Lane
Port Orchard, WA 98366
206 227–5878
www.steve-keating.com
steve@steve-keating.com
pp. 5 (2nd.), 38–41, 58, 64, 65 (Bot L & R),
66 (L & Top R), Courtesy of Balance
Architects (see Contributors)

Kraftmaid Cabinetry
pp. 5 (4th.), 32, 54, 57, 98–99, 101,
104–107, 114–115, 162–163, Courtesy
of Kraftmaid Cabinetry (see Contributors)

Joseph Lapeyra Photography
4611 S. University Drive
Davie, FL 33328–3817
954 680–4910
www.lapeyraphoto.com
joe@lapeyraphoto.com
pp. 63 (Top), 74–75, 81 (R), 90, Courtesy of
Sater Design (see Contributors)

Tom Lenchek
pp. 59, 65 (Top L & R), 66 (Bot R), 67,
Courtesy of Balance Architects (see
Contributors)

Kathryn MacDonald Photography
690 Fifth Street, Suite 107
San Francisco, CA 94107
415 371–8300
www.macdonaldphoto.com
pp. 24–25, 42–43, Courtesy of Philip J.
Meyer LTD Interior Design (see
Contributors)

Manhattan Cabinetry
pp. 21, 143, Courtesy of Manhattan
Cabinetry (see Contributors)

Robert Millman
P.O. Box 3566
Aspen, CO 81612
970 923–6511
www.robertmillman.com
robert@robertmillman.com
pp. 26–27, Courtesy of Seidel/Holzman
Architects (see Contributors)

Kim Sargent Photography
7675 Steeplechase Drive
Palm Beach Gardens, FL 33418
561 881–8887
www.sargentphoto.com
sargentphoto@att.net
pp. 55, 63 (Bot), 80, 82, 87, Courtesy of
Sater Design (see Contributors)

Doug Thompson Photography
24506 Dolphin Street
Bonita Springs, FL 34134
239 922–5639
www.dougthompson.net
doug@dougthompson.net
pp. 5 (1st.), 6–7, 10–15, 19–20, 28–29, 61,
76–79, 92, 94–97, 164 (L), 165, Courtesy
of Sater Design (see Contributors)

©John Vaughn & Associates
510 583–8075
maria@jvaughan.com
p. 91, Courtesy of Seidel/Holzman
Architects (see Contributors)

CJ Walker Photography
717 Flamingo Drive
West Palm Beach, FL 33401
561 659–2457
www.cjwalker.com
cjw@cjwalker.com
p. 84, Courtesy of Sater Design
(see Contributors)

Whirlpool Corporation

Whirlpool® Home Appliances
pp. 127, 134 (Bot L), 146, 147(L),
Courtesy of Whirlpool Corporation
(see Contributors)

Gladiator GarageWorks®
pp. 118–119, 121 (Top R & Bot L & R),
Courtesy of Whirlpool Corporation
(see Contributors)

KitchenAid® Home Appliances
pp. 134 (Top L), 135–136, 138, 162,
Courtesy of Whirlpool Corporation
(see Contributors)

Victor Wong Photography
P.O. Box 14553
San Francisco, CA 94114–0553
victor@vwphotosudio.com
415 934–8618
pp. 34–35, Courtesy of Group 41 Inc.
(see Contributors)

Wood-Mode Inc.
pp. 102–103, 112–113
Courtesy of Wood-Mode Inc. (see
Contributors)

Index